THE MOUNTAINS AROUND NERJA

SCENIC WALKS IN SOUTHERN ANDALUCÍA – SIERRAS TEJEDA, ALMIJARA AND ALHAMA

by Jim Ryan

JUNIPER HOUSE, MURLEY MOSS,
OXENHOLME ROAD, KENDAL, CUMBRIA LA9 7RL
www.cicerone.co.uk

© Jim Ryan 2024
Second edition 2024
ISBN: 978 1 78631 176 4
First edition 2014

Printed in Singapore by KHL Printing on responsibly sourced paper.
A catalogue record for this book is available from the British Library.
All photographs are by the author unless otherwise stated.

Route mapping by Lovell Johns www.lovelljohns.com
Contains OpenStreetMap.org data © OpenStreetMap contributors, CC-BY-SA. NASA relief data courtesy of ESRI

Acknowledgements

This guidebook is dedicated to the people of Nerja and surrounding towns and villages from whom I have derived tremendous camaraderie, friendship and cooperation. My late wife, Sue, was my inspiration and she proofread the first edition. My wife, Birgit, is my companion both at home and in the mountains. I was very fortunate to marry a woman who has lived in Cómpeta and Nerja for over 30 years and knows every dirt track through the sierra. It is she who appears in many of the images in this book.

Updates to this guide

While every effort is made by our authors to ensure the accuracy of guidebooks as they go to print, changes can occur during the lifetime of an edition. Any updates that we know of for this guide will be on the Cicerone website (www.cicerone.co.uk/1176/updates), so please check before planning your trip. We also advise that you check information about such things as transport, accommodation and shops locally. Even rights of way can be altered over time. We are always grateful for information about any discrepancies between a guidebook and the facts on the ground, sent by email to updates@cicerone.co.uk or by post to Cicerone, Juniper House, Murley Moss, Oxenholme Road, Kendal, LA9 7RL.
  Register your book: To sign up to receive free updates, special offers and GPX files where available, create a Cicerone account and register your purchase via the 'My Account' tab at www.cicerone.co.uk.

Front cover: The white village of Frigiliana nestles under the peak of Lucero

CONTENTS

Route summary table 6
Preface 9

INTRODUCTION 11
Walking in Andalucía 12
Geographical context 14
A little history 19
Wildlife 21
Getting to Nerja 22
Accommodation 23
When to go 23
What to take 25
Language 25
Maps and GPS 26
Using this guide 27

THE WALKS 29
Nerja and around 30
Walk 1   Frigiliana to Nerja via Fuente del Esparto 31
Walk 2   El Fuerte from Frigiliana 37
Walk 3   El Fuerte from El Acebuchal 44
Walk 4   La Cruz del Pinto 47
Walk 5   The Gorges of the Río Chillar 51
Walk 6   El Cielo circuit 55
Walk 7   The tour of Almendrón 59
Walk 8   Navachica 64
The Cómpeta area 68
Walk 9   La Fábrica de la Luz 69
Walk 10 Lucero 72
Walk 11 Cerro de la Chapa 75
Walk 12 The oak forest of Salares 78
Walk 13 Cómpeta to Los Pradillos 81
Walk 14 Malascamas from La Fábrica de la Luz 86
La Maroma 90
Walk 15 La Maroma from Salares 93
Walk 16 La Maroma from Canillas de Aceituno 96
Walk 17 La Maroma from Alcaucín 100
Walk 18 La Maroma from Sedella 103

Walk 19	La Maroma from Alcaicería	106
Walk 20	Canillas de Aceituno to the cable bridge	109
Walk 21	Sedella to the cable bridge	112
Walk 22	Torrecilla de La Maroma	116
Walks from the east		119
Walk 23	El Cielo from Valle de la Miel	120
Walk 24	The Petrified Waterfall	124
Walk 25	Lopera	128
Walks from the north		132
Walk 26	Pico del Puerto	133
Walk 27	The hole in the mountain	136
Walk 28	Malascamas via Barranco de Malinfierno	138
Walk 29	The Gorge of Alhama de Granada	143
Walk 30	La Resinera	147
Walk 31	Malascamas from Robledal	150
Cisne		154
Walk 32	Cisne from El Acebuchal	155

Appendix A	List of peaks by altitude	159
Appendix B	Wild mountain flowers of Andalucía	160
Appendix C	Glossary of useful Spanish words	167
Appendix D	Further reading	168
Appendix E	Useful contacts	170

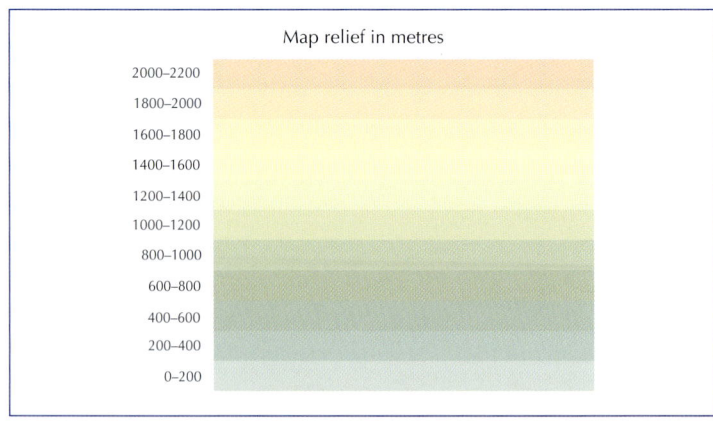

Mountain safety

Every mountain walk has its dangers, and those described in this guidebook are no exception. All who walk or climb in the mountains should recognise this and take responsibility for themselves and their companions along the way. The author and publisher have made every effort to ensure that the information contained in this guide was correct when it went to press, but, except for any liability that cannot be excluded by law, they cannot accept responsibility for any loss, injury or inconvenience sustained by any person using this book.

International distress signal *(emergency only)*
Six blasts on a whistle (and flashes with a torch after dark) spaced evenly for one minute, followed by a minute's pause. Repeat until an answer is received. The response is three signals per minute followed by a minute's pause.

Helicopter rescue
The following signals are used to communicate with a helicopter:

Help needed:
raise both arms
above head to
form a 'Y'

Help not needed:
raise one arm
above head, extend
other arm downward

Emergency telephone numbers
To call out Mountain Rescue, ring the international emergency number 112 – this will connect you via any available network.
The telephone number for the police throughout Spain is 091.

Weather reports
Nerja weather forecast: www.nerjatoday.com/nerjanews/nerja-weather or
www.accuweather.com

Mountain rescue can be very expensive – be adequately insured.

The Mountains around Nerja

ROUTE SUMMARY TABLE

Walk	Name	Start/Finish	Distance	Time	Height gain	Difficulty	Page
Nerja and around							
1	Frigiliana to Nerja via Fuente del Esparto	Frigiliana/ Cave of Nerja	14km	5hr	605m	4	31
2	El Fuerte from Frigiliana	Frigiliana	8.5km	3hr 30min	670m	4	37
3	El Fuerte from El Acebuchal	El Acebuchal	8km	4hr 30min	510m	7	44
4	La Cruz del Pinto	Nerja	8km	4hr 30min	370m	2	47
5	The Gorges of the Río Chillar	Nerja	15km	4hr	340m	3	51
6	El Cielo circuit	nr El Pinarillo recreation area	14km	7hr	1180m	8	55
7	The tour of Almendrón	nr El Pinarillo recreation area	12km	6hr	930m	9	59
8	Navachica	nr El Pinarillo recreation area	15km	8hr	1485m	7	64
The Cómpeta area							
9	La Fábrica de la Luz	Fábrica de la Luz	13km	4hr	530m	2	69
10	Lucero	off the road to Fábrica de la Luz	10.5km	4hr 30min	730m	5	72

ROUTE SUMMARY TABLE

Walk	Name	Start/Finish	Distance	Time	Height gain	Difficulty	Page
11	Cerro de la Chapa	off the road to Fábrica de la Luz	11km	5hr	600m	4	75
12	The oak forest of Salares	Salares	7.5km	3hr	315m	2	78
13	Cómpeta to Los Pradillos	nr Cómpeta	14km	4hr	410m	3	81
14	Malascamas from La Fábrica de la Luz	Fábrica de la Luz	22km	7hr 30min	1135m	8	86
La Maroma							
15	La Maroma from Salares	nr Salares	12km	4hr 30min	560m	5	93
16	La Maroma from Canillas de Aceituno	Canillas de Aceituno	18km	7hr	1420m	6	96
17	La Maroma from Alcaucín	El Alcázar (nr Alcaucín)	16km	6hr 30min	1225m	7	100
18	La Maroma from Sedella	Sedella recreation area	17km	7hr	1245m	7	103
19	La Maroma from Alcaicería	Robledal (nr Alcaicería)	15km	6hr	960m	6	106
20	Canillas de Aceituno to the cable bridge	Canillas de Aceituno	10km	3hr 30min	210m	3	109
21	Sedella to the cable bridge	Sedella recreation area	8km	3hr 30min	475m	5	112
22	Torrecilla de La Maroma	Alcaucín	15km	5hr 30min	1005m	5	116

THE MOUNTAINS AROUND NERJA

Walk	Name	Start/Finish	Distance	Time	Height gain	Difficulty	Page
Walks from the east							
23	El Cielo from Valle de la Miel	Valle de la Miel	11km	6hr 30min	1080m	5	120
24	The Petrified Waterfall	A-4050 (16km beyond Otívar)	11km	4hr	410m	4	124
25	Lopera	A-4050 (22km beyond Otívar)	8.7km	3hr	275m	1	128
Walks from the north							
26	Pico del Puerto	Ventas de Zafarraya	6km	3hr	355m	4	133
27	The hole in the mountain	Ventas de Zafarraya	3km	1hr 30min	265m	3	136
28	Malascamas via Barranco de Malinfierno	off A-1450 (nr Jatar)	17.5km	7hr	865m	6	138
29	The Gorge of Alhama de Granada	Alhama de Granada	6km	2hr 30min	110m	1	143
30	La Resinera	Fornes	11km	3hr	235m	1	147
31	Malascamas from Robledal	Robledal (nr Alcaicería)	16km	6hr 30min	955m	5	150
Cisne							
32	Cisne from El Acebuchal	El Acebuchal	16km	8hr	1150m	10	155

Starting the descent of La Maroma (Walks 15–19)

PREFACE

The Spanish are attentive and invest in outdoor pursuits as part of their policy of 'Sport for All'. In 2020 the province of Málaga launched its *Gran Senda de Málaga*, the Great Path of Málaga. This 700km series of walks is spread throughout the province and includes some of the walks in this guidebook. The Gran Senda de Málaga is one of the main reasons for the need to update this guidebook, for it has altered waymarked walks, established new trails and enhanced the attraction of Málaga as a venue for hillwalking.

The number of walks in this edition has increased from 24 to 32, and entirely new maps have been created, utilising OpenStreetMap data. We have also added an appendix on the wild mountain flowers of Andalucía.

The gorge of Alhama de Granada (Walk 29)

INTRODUCTION

Dirt track on the return from the Petrified Waterfall (Walk 24)

The little seaside town of Nerja nestles under a range of mighty mountains that stretch to the north, away from the coast. Hillwalkers internationally have begun to realise what treasures lie in this region. Although these mountains are well known locally in Spain, the neighbouring mountains of the Alpujarras and the Sierra Nevada to the east have up until now been the better recognised attractions for the outdoor fraternity of northern Europe.

However, by 2011, the ever-increasing numbers of visitors coming to the Sierras Tejeda, Almijara and Alhama led the government of Andalucía to build a state-of-the-art interpretive centre at Sedella in the south and expand the interpretive centre near Fornes in the north, and their 2011 guide to the area (in Spanish) is now widely distributed.

Today, walkers with their boots, rucksacks and walking sticks are a common sight in the town of Nerja and the neighbouring villages of Cómpeta, Frigiliana and Canillas de Albaida.

In 2020, recognising the resource they had, and as a commitment to sport for all, the government commissioned the GR 249 *Gran Senda de Málaga* – Great Path of Málaga – 700km of walks in 35 stages. These walks are all waymarked, with information boards and are all maintained. In order to complete the walk between the villages of Canillas de Aceituno and Sedella a suspension bridge was built at a cost of €630,000, a bridge so spectacular that it draws crowds of sightseers every weekend. A free 200-page Spanish-language guidebook has been produced for the GR 249. Of course, only a small part of

THE MOUNTAINS AROUND NERJA

the GR 249 is in the Parque Natural de las Sierras Tejeda, Almijara y Alhama – the mountains around Nerja.

Here there are more than 55 mountains over 914m (3000ft, equivalent to the Scottish Munros) in an area about the size of the Isle of Skye. The highest of these mountains is over 2000m, and a significant number are taller than Ben Nevis. Many of the mountains have maintained and waymarked paths.

To climb the mountains of Scotland and Ireland hillwalkers need to consider that the summit will be in cloud 70 to 80 per cent of the time; by contrast, in Andalucía this figure is more like ten per cent. Spain is also one of the most affordable countries in Europe to visit and there is a universal welcome for the visitor.

The aim of this guide is to provide accurate information and route directions for independent walkers, with lots of background information to make their explorations of this stunning area even more rewarding.

WALKING IN ANDALUCÍA

The Andalucían Parque Nacional has set up and now maintains designated walking trails, and many of the walks in this book follow such trails. The paths are often old mining routes or former mule tracks through the mountains. All of these maintained paths are waymarked. They have a sign at the start of the walk (in Spanish) with notes on what you are about to encounter, a little history, the distance and time it will take and the relative difficulty. It is important to note that the time given on these signs is always for a one-way trip and does not include your return to the start.

WALKING IN ANDALUCÍA

The waymarks indicate the direction; where other paths link there are waymarks with crosses to show that they are not to be followed. All waymarked paths have relatively moderate gradients. For the experienced walker this can be a little frustrating because the route is extended to maintain the gentle gradient and can become laboriously long. In this book shortcuts have been adopted for the most excessive cases.

Many of the walks are not on waymarked trails, which tend to make them more challenging. Over time paths can be subject to change: from earthworks, landslides, river flooding, vegetation encroachment and so on, so that you need to keep your wits about you.

The most important thing is to find the start of the path and be sure that it is the correct path. Once you are on a path all you need to do is follow it. Wandering off the path is generally not an option because of the surrounding vegetation.

Typical waymarker

The Almijara mountains above the town of Nerja (L: western; R: eastern)

Lucerillo 1690m
Lucero 1779m
La Cruz del Pinto 365m
Cisne 1491m

The Mountains around Nerja

Waymarkers for stages of the GR 249 Gran Senda de Málaga included in the walks are red and white. Local waymarkers are slightly different, some with yellow and white markings and others not coloured at all.

Almost all the land in this area is in public ownership and is part of the national park. The exceptions are areas immediately north of Frigiliana, part of the Río Verde Valley, the eastern walk of Ventas de Zafarraya, and land north of La Maroma. There are signs indicating when land is private and none of the routes in this book require you to trespass on private land where it is so indicated.

GEOGRAPHICAL CONTEXT

Nerja is a small coastal town 60km east of Málaga, presided over to the north by the Almijaras. The Almijaras are orientated on an east–west axis and they join the Sierra Tejeda to the west and the smaller Sierra Alhama further to the northwest. There are three other minor sierras on the periphery of the region. The foothills of the Sierra Nevada, the Alpujarras, are some 80km to the northeast.

The wider region in which the routes described in this book sit is referred to in Spanish as the Axarquía, which comes from Moorish and means the lands to the east. The principal towns of the Axarquía are Vélez-Málaga and Nerja, but Nerja is the one chosen as the focus of this guide because it is closest to the centre of the mountains, and many of the walks included begin there. The official name for the area, promoted by the Andalucían Tourist Board, is Sierras Tejeda, Almijara y Alhama, which is also the name of the publicly owned natural park.

The town of Nerja

Nerja has a population of 22,000, which grows in the summer to several times this number with the influx of tourists. Many of the properties in the town are unoccupied outside the tourist season. The town is well known throughout Spain because *Verano Azul*, a popular soap opera on Spanish television some years ago, was based here. Today 20 per cent of the permanent residents of Nerja are foreigners who have relocated mainly from northern Europe, typically England, Sweden, Germany, the Netherlands, Ireland and Belgium.

The town is a maze of narrow streets that all seem to lead towards the *Balcón de Europa*, a public square on a promontory above the Mediterranean.

There is no beach of any size in the centre of town, but on the outskirts, to the east and west, there are fine beaches. Nerja boasts many quality, medium-priced hotels, hostels and apartments to rent, and there are numerous excellent restaurants, bars and nightclubs. Most of the hotels cater for group bookings and there are discounts in the off-peak seasons.

GEOGRAPHICAL CONTEXT

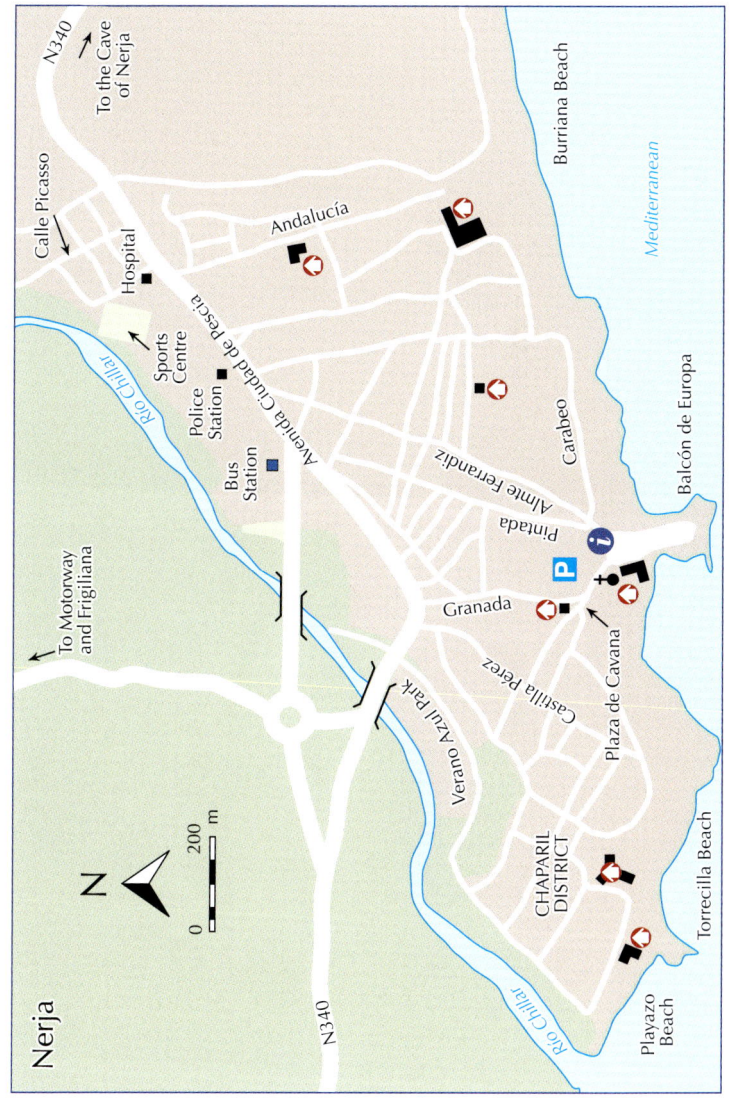

Dawn on the beach under the Balcón de Europa

One of the principal tourist attractions is the Cave of Nerja. Situated immediately northeast of the town, this limestone cave has 5km of chambers, many of magnificent proportions, which were inhabited as far back as 25,000 years ago.

The white mountain villages

Frigiliana, Cómpeta, Canillas de Albaida, Canillas de Aceituno and Salares are just some of the quaint, white-painted villages a short distance from Nerja. Several others are visited on the walks. These villages have a history that spans the occupations by the Romans and the Moors and they still pursue old customs and a pace of life that reflects the traditions of rural Spain.

Street in El Acebuchal (Walk 3)

GEOGRAPHICAL CONTEXT

Geology and topography

The mountains around Nerja are largely limestone, but they span 500 million years of geological time. The youngest rocks are the conglomerates that can be seen below the Balcón de Europa, which are only 10,000 years old. The cliffs of Alhama de Granada (Walk 29) are from the Miocene and so are about 15 million years old. For the climb at Ventas de Zafarraya (Walks 26 and 27), it's a jump back in time to the Jurassic rocks, 180 million years old. But the oldest limestones are those that form the main body of the mountains around Nerja and these are between 280 and 500 million years old, spanning geological periods from the Permian back through the Carboniferous and into the Cambrian.

The older rocks were lifted and the mountains substantially formed 30 million years ago during the tectonic collision of a Mediterranean breakaway plate with the land masses of Africa and Europe. This collision caused the formation of the Betic Cordillera of which Sierra Nevada, the Alpujarras and the mountains around Nerja are a part.

The limestone varies from white soft chalk to hard, blue calcitic rocks. In the area of Fuente del Esparto there are lenses of black limestone shales, while near Lucero the heat from the mountain building has turned the limestone into marble. There are no volcanic rocks in this region. There are areas where the limestone is friable, reminiscent of the Dolomites, and other areas where they are karstic, with holes cut into the rock by acidic solution. The entire area is dotted with caves of all shapes and sizes.

The mountains consist of a main chain stretching from La Maroma (2069m) in the west through Cerro Santiago (1645m), Malascamas (1793m), Cerro de la Chapa (1818m), Lucero (1779m) and La Cadena (1645m) to Navachica (1831m) and Lopera (1485m) in the east. South of the main chain is a series of foothills of which El Fuerte (976m), Tres Cruces (1204m) and Cerro Atalaya (1255m) are examples. At Navachica the mountain range opens into a three-pronged fork with Cerro Cisne (1483m) on the western limb, Tajo de Almendrón (1515m) in the middle and El Cielo (1508m) on the eastern limb.

Earthquakes

The convergence of the African and Eurasian tectonic plates (estimated at 5mm per annum) causes regular earthquakes in southeast Spain and northwest Africa. Earthquakes of magnitude 4 and above on the Richter scale are detected in Nerja on average every two weeks, and quakes that shake and damage buildings might be expected every five years. The most damaging quake in relatively recent times was on Christmas Day in 1884 when a tremor measuring 6.5 on the Richter scale, with its epicentre northeast of Canillas de Aceituno, affected every

THE MOUNTAINS AROUND NERJA

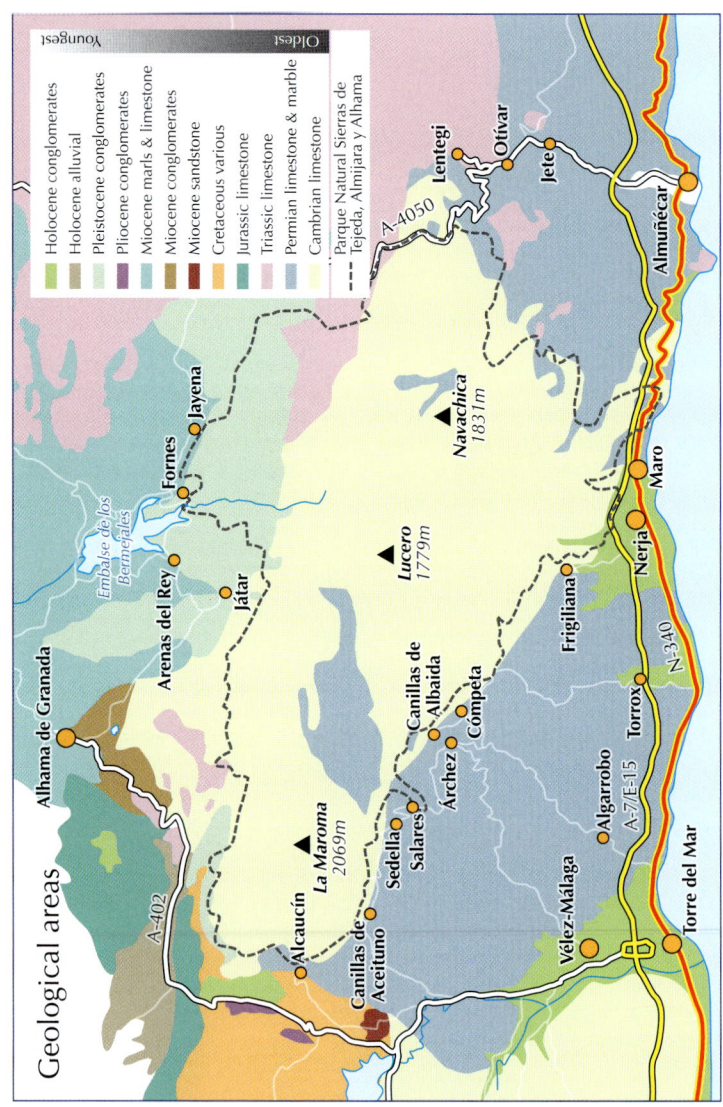

Malascamas summit, with La Maroma in the distance (Walks 14, 28 and 31)

village and town in the Axarquía, killing 745 people. Further tremors occurred in January and minor aftershocks were felt throughout the following year. The devastation was compounded by heavy snows in the mountains. More recently, a minor quake shook the town in 2016, but little damage was caused.

A LITTLE HISTORY

Spanish history is extremely complex and very difficult to summarise so only a brief overview can be given here.

Early evidence of human beings in Spain was found in 1933 in a cave near Zafarraya. Bones were discovered that are believed to have belonged to Neanderthal man, dating to 30,000 years ago.

There is also evidence of prehistoric life in the Cave of Nerja. Near Fornes in the extreme north of the region there is a passage grave that has been dated to the Neolithic period. The Iberian Peninsula is known to have been visited by the Phoenicians and in 2023 excavations were underway on Mesa de Fornes, exposing the ruins of Phoenician buildings. The Greeks were the next to visit, before the arrival of the Romans, some 200 years BC. Hispania, as it was then known, was ruled from Rome for 600 years.

From around AD400 to AD700 the peninsula was conquered by the Visigoths, who were subsequently replaced by the Moors. These Muslims ruled Spain until the early 13th century, when the Catholic Conquest

Roman bridge near Alhama de Granada

began. In the Axarquía there was considerable Moorish influence. It can be seen today in the Alhambra in Granada. Mudéjar architecture is widespread and all towns and villages with names beginning with 'al' betray their Moorish origins. The climate in Andalucía was ideal for the silk industry established by the Moors. Even to this day Arabic features are more evident in the people of Andalucía than in those of the rest of Spain.

During the Moorish period there were three main religious groups – the Muslims, the Christians and the Jews. The Jews allied themselves to the Muslims and lived in close proximity to them as their protectors from the Christians. After the Catholic Conquest all people were required to convert to Christianity or face death or expulsion. The majority of the Muslims did so convert and were then known as *Moriscos*, but the Jews were forced to leave the country.

From late in the 19th century to the beginning of World War 2, Spain was torn between disputes over the monarchy, a republic and dictatorship. During the Spanish Civil War and for years after it in Andalucía, and particularly in the Axarquía district, there were many enclaves of Republicans who resisted the dictator General Franco, and there were numerous bloody encounters. The mountains visited on the walks in this book were ideal refuges for the Maquis, the Republican sympathisers, to hide in.

WILDLIFE

Birds and animals

The wildlife and plants of the Spanish hillsides are truly remarkable and very different from those of northern Europe. There are very few dangerous creatures about, and where there are they will be as nervous of you as you are of them.

The *cabra montés* is only found in the Iberian Peninsula and mostly in the Axarquía. You will frequently get a glimpse of these wild goats with deerskin hides, but they are very shy and will move away from intruders. They are also extremely agile and will often be seen travelling up and down slopes at great speed. Although it would be unusual to come across a wild boar (*jabalí*), you might see disturbed ground where they have been digging for soft roots and grubs. In the area around La Resinera, you may also encounter red deer.

Seeing wild cats, foxes and hares will be a rarity. Similarly, snakes are shy and infrequently encountered. There are many birds of prey to be spotted hovering in the skies, including kestrels, falcons, vultures and even eagles.

Processionary caterpillars are the most dangerous insects in Spain. They make their woven white cocoons in the branches of pine trees and descend to the ground, where they wander in lines that may be several metres in length until they find a hole or cave to settle in. However docile they may seem, they carry a nasty poison on their hairy backs. When humans (or their dogs) come into contact with these hairs, they can cause reactions ranging from mild inflammation and irritation to severe anaphylactic shock. If you get any reaction from contact with these insects medical advice should be sought.

Processionary caterpillars about to descend from a pine tree, having disposed of their white cocoon

Plants and flowers

The mountain flowers come to life in the spring, when many familiar species and others that are particular to the Mediterranean will be better seen. The exotic *flor de jara* thrives on the slopes of these mountains. This bush, related to the *cistus* (rock rose), likes the lime-rich soil. Where the Spanish name for a plant or flower mentioned in the route descriptions is available it is given, and some of these are very interesting. For example broom, which is called *lluvia de oro* (rain of gold).

The most common tree to be seen on these walks is the pine tree. However, in the past yew trees predominated here. Sierra Tejeda takes its name from the Spanish word for yew, *tejo*. The yews were cut down because they were considered to be poisonous to livestock and pines were planted in their place to expand the resin industry. The demise of the yews is highlighted in the interpretive centres and a programme has commenced to replace some of them. The pines are well adapted to withstand drought. The red-berried prickly juniper features on many of the walks and you will also come across the holm oak – the evergreen holly oak – which has adapted here to survive the dry summers.

See Appendix B for an illustrated guide to the wild mountain flowers of the region. If you want to read more about Spanish wildflowers in general, two field guides are recommended in Appendix D.

GETTING TO NERJA

Nerja is a one-hour bus ride from Málaga, a city well served by rail and bus from the remainder of Spain – particularly via the cities of Madrid, Seville and Cádiz – and Portugal, and thence from Europe. Spanish train timetables can be checked and tickets bought online at www.renfe.com and bus times and tickets are available at www.alsa.es.

The airport at Málaga is one of the busiest in Spain with flights into it from almost every country in Europe. Easyjet (www.easyjet.com), Ryanair (www.ryanair.com), British Airways (www.britishairways.co.uk) and Aer Lingus (www.aerlingus.com) all operate regular flights to Málaga from various cities in the UK and Ireland. From outside the airport terminal there is a regular train and bus service into the centre of Málaga, where regular buses run from the main bus station to Nerja. The fares on these buses are remarkably cheap. Málaga Shuttle Bus was an excellent alternative, but, at time of publication, had not resumed after the pandemic.

Nerja is 40 minutes by car from Málaga. A taxi to and from the airport, arranged beforehand, is a little expensive (€70 in 2023) but, shared with others, can be convenient. The airport at Almería to the east is more than an hour from Nerja and is not served as well with buses and car rentals.

Hiring a car

Out of the summer season, hiring a car can be remarkably cheap. Malagacar (www.malagacar.com) is a very efficient operator. They hold the largest fleet of cars in the area. If you are hiring a car, consider the option of hiring an SUV. Mini SUVs, such as the Seat Arona, Renault Captur and VW T-Cross, cost virtually the same as a standard saloon of the same size. Their higher road clearance makes them more suitable for off-road driving, which is essential for the approach to some of the routes, particularly Walk 15.

ACCOMMODATION

Each of the routes in this guide could be done in a single day trip from Nerja, so Nerja is a good place to base yourself. There are hotels in Nerja that specialise in group bookings for walkers. Since walkers generally come in the spring or autumn, out-of-season rates apply. These hotels operate on a bed, breakfast, packed lunch and evening meal basis, or on variations of these.

The hotels specialising in catering for walking groups tend to be medium to small hotels, but there are a few luxury establishments in the town as well. Equally, there are hostels that are economic and operate on a bed and breakfast arrangement. A useful source of information about accommodation in Nerja is www.nerjatoday.com.

For those who want to fend for themselves, Nerja has many empty apartments available to rent in the off season. Almost all of the real estate agencies in the town provide this service. The option of renting and eating out is very practical, for there are numerous cafés and restaurants that open early and serve anything from coffee and rolls to a full English breakfast. For evening meals there is a wide choice – English roasts, Italian pastas, Indian curries, spicy Mexican dishes and many fine establishments serving the best of Spanish cuisine.

The choice of accommodation location lies between proximity to the town centre, the beaches and the mountains. Nerja town centre is a maze of narrow one-way streets and is decidedly not car-friendly. So, cars may have to be parked away from your accommodation.

The bus from Málaga arrives at the top, or eastern, end of the town. It is a 10-minute, downhill walk to most places within the town, but there is a taxi rank at the bus station.

WHEN TO GO

Officially it never rains in Nerja during June, July and August, at least not in living memory. However, as well as being dry during these months, the weather is hot and the town is packed with tourists. In this high season everything is that little bit more expensive. While the coast is basking in heat the mountains tend to be shrouded

Snow on the ascent to La Maroma (Walks 15–19 and 21)

in cloud. The Nerjans say that the town has its own microclimate such that it never gets unbearably hot and does not suffer from the high humidity of other coastal towns. The coldest months are January and February when the temperature at night could be as low as 10ºC, but during the day it could rise to the high teens. Rain will fall any time between November and March, but a whole day's rain is rather unusual.

For hillwalkers, the best time to go is January through to early May. There may be a little snow on La Maroma, but otherwise the temperature is ideal for walking: not too hot and with little threat of rain. The flowers will be in full bloom and the landscape will be green. In early March the flowers will be out, but the rainy season will not have concluded. The two biggest festivals in the town take place over Easter and on 15 May. Religious processions are big throughout Andalucía, when a significant proportion of the townsfolk take part. Spanish tourists pour into the town to witness the dedication that the community has to its processions. The spectacle is a moving one.

In autumn and early winter the weather will again be very suitable for walking, but after the hot summer the land will be brown and scorched. From November through to February walking in Andalucía is still very acceptable, although you are more likely to get rain and possibly snow on La Maroma. There will be more water in the rivers, many of which must be crossed on the walks, so that getting your feet wet may become inevitable. Snow on the Almijaras is rare, but it is most likely on Navachica. There is never any snow on the slopes of Lucero because the high winds remove it, but there can be snow on the northern approach to its summit.

The dirt-track road into Pinarillo and Fuente del Esparto is generally closed from 1 June to 1 October, because of the threat of forest fires.

In particularly dry periods it may also be closed in November. This is not an insignificant factor for walkers, since it adds considerably to the length of several walks. The normal route to the mountain of El Cielo (Walk 6), which is the most dominant peak seen from Nerja, uses that dirt track into Pinarillo (if closed, Walk 23 provides an alternative route from the east).

WHAT TO TAKE

The paths and terrain are all quite rough, so sturdy boots are recommended. Since there is no wet or boggy ground, gaiters are not necessary. If you plan to ascend La Maroma (only from the north) between December and February, crampons will be necessary, but the short-studded, elasticated ones (microspikes) will suffice. Sunshine is going to be more of an issue than inclement weather. A shell jacket should always be in the bottom of your rucksack, but there should be no need to bring waterproof pants. The emphasis should be on light, dry-flow clothes, as opposed to warm shirts and fleeces. However, on windy days in mid-winter, it would be wise to bring gloves and a light fleece. Each of the walks provides advice on the vegetation: where the route is through dense vegetation it may be advisable to wear lightweight trousers rather than shorts. Factor 50 sunscreen and a sunhat will be essential. Walkers are advised to use sticks, especially on descents.

During hot months in the mountains it is essential to bring enough water or other fluid ('enough' will vary from person to person but 1–2 litres per person is a good rule of thumb when exerting yourself in a hot climate). Water sources on the walks are generally poor to non-existent.

You could encounter snakes on any of the walks in this book but it is highly unlikely. They will be more scared of you than you are of them and will keep well away if they can. However, it may be wise to wear gaiters in areas of thick vegetation. For the walk on El Cielo, in particular, ankle protection is recommended, because you will not be able to see the ground clearly on the first half of the walk.

The routes in this book are not technical. The only walk for which roping up is recommended is the ascent of Cisne, at the point of the traverse on the eastern side of the summit.

Likewise, a GPS is not necessary for most of the walks in this book. However, you should take one if you are going to tackle the walks to Almendrón (Walk 7), Navachica (Walk 8), Malascamas (Walk 28) and Cisne (Walk 32).

LANGUAGE

A glossary of useful Spanish words for map reading can be found in Appendix C. For convenience, a summary of this guidebook's most frequently occurring terms is provided below:

FREQUENTLY USED WORDS

barranco	ravine
cerro	mountain, hill
collado	col
cortijo	country farmhouse
mirador	viewpoint
rifugio	refuge
sendero	path
venta	inn, hostelry

Spanish dialect in Andalucía

There are many peculiarities in the speech of Andalucíans that differentiate it from the *Castellaño* that is spoken in Madrid. The language sounds much smoother here, not as harsh as that of the northern neighbours and more akin to the Spanish of South America.

For example, the word 'Andalucía' is pronounced as it would be in English, whereas in Madrid it would be 'Andalu**th**ía'. The English pronunciation of the name 'Nerja' is 'Ner**k**a', but to be more correct it is 'Ner**h**a', with the 'h' pronounced gutterally.

The river that flows through the town is the Río Chillar, which is pronounced 'Chiyar' because two 'l's are pronounced as a 'y' in Spanish.

In Andalucía there is a tendency to drop the letter 's' from the middle and ending of words. So to buy two beers (*dos cervezas*) the request in Madrid would be 'dos thervethas'. In Nerja, 'do cervayza' will be heard, or for three it will be 'tray'. To ask how a person is one would say ¿*cómo estás?* in Madrid, but in Nerja it would be '¿cómo **aytá**?', both of the 's's having been dropped.

The Spanish pronounce all their vowels individually. So the unit of currency is an '**a**yuro'.

Recurring place names

There is a degree of repetition in the names of geographical features. There are two Puerto Blanquillos and a Puerta Blanquilla; there are at least two Salto de Caballos, two El Fuerte mountains and a couple of Cerro Verdes; one set of peaks is known as Los Dos Hermanos (the two brothers), a col on Cisne is known as Collado de Dos Hermanos, while another peak is called Las Dos Hermanas (the two sisters). To the north of the region there is the town of Arenas del Rey, while nearer the coast there is the village of Arenas. But as long as you know where you are, there should be no cause for confusion!

MAPS AND GPS

Mapa Topográfico de España, on behalf of the Junta de Andalucía, publish 1:50,000 and 1:25,000 maps of the area laid out to the 1950 European UTM grid. These maps are relatively inexpensive to buy but are not widely available. The quality of paper is poor and all paths are not shown on them. For some of the walks more than one

LOCAL WALKING CLUBS

Every town and village in the general area has a walking club or association, and you can find contact details on the internet. However, the conversation will always be in Spanish. The Nerja walking club is La Gineta Club de Montaña. At time of publication its secretary was Fernando Arce, and his telephone number was +34 609 5232 35 (Spanish language only). The walks that this club organises are generally challenging.

Bautista Atencia is a member of the Nerja Gineta Walking Club and has been walking these mountains for over fifty years

map will be required. They can be purchased direct at a shop in Málaga (Mapas y Compañía), or they can be purchased online (see Appendix D).

Editorial Penebética publish a 1:40,000 map that covers the area. It shows walks on the map and provides a booklet describing each walk (Spanish only). The alternative Piolet map is at a scale of 1:25,000 and is printed on two sheets. It shows 34 tracks, with no accompanying booklet.

The *Axarquía Tour and Trail* 1:40,000 published by Discovery Walking Guides is quite a clear map, but the October 2010 version has many little mistakes (for instance, Frigiliana and Canillas de Aceituno are misspelled, and there are a number of features that are out of place). Unfortunately, the 2010 version is to an imperial grid.

Most people take smartphones with map apps on them, and some of these provide GPS coordinates. There is often not a great deal of point, therefore, in giving waypoint coordinates. The important instructions are those that lead to the start of the walk and help you stick to the path. Wandering off the path is often impossible due to the thick vegetation.

Once you have purchased this guidebook you may download the walks from the Cicerone website (www.cicerone.co.uk/1176/GPX) onto your mobile device. It is advisable to do this for walks that have difficult navigational sections.

USING THIS GUIDE

All the walks are designed to be completed during a day trip from Nerja, and directions to the start of all walks are given from the town of Nerja. Some summary information is provided before the start of each route description to help you select the right walk for you and your party. This includes total distance, total height gain – cumulative metres gained during the entire walk – a rough estimate of the time it might take (allowing for regular rest stops and refreshment breaks), a difficulty rating and directions for getting to the start of the walk. The latter includes a three-word code, for example ///bonanza.venues.saucer, that can be entered on the free app (and website) What3Words to give a precise location for the walk start. Other options for your day in that particular area are also suggested in some cases. There is also a Route summary table to help you compare the different walks.

Route maps

The routes are marked onto 1:50,000 base maps, except for detailed navigation through villages, where street maps are provided. The main route is in red and variants are dashed.

GPX tracks for the routes in this guidebook are available to download free at www.cicerone.co.uk/1176/GPX. All the official Spanish mapping is also now available to buy digitally, by map title, province or region, for use on navigation apps on tablets, phones and other devices.

Walkers will find the apps OutdoorActive and Komoot useful for navigation. The former uses OpenStreetMap on which the GPX files are based. Komoot shows more clearly which roads are paved, dirt-tracks, or mere narrow paths. Additionally, this guide provides precise locations of the start of the walks using the app What3Words.

Difficulty

The difficulty rating given for each route is on a scale of one to ten, with the higher numbers reserved for long, strenuous and more challenging walks. A route with a difficulty rating of 1 would be suitable for children and elderly people and where ordinary sports shoes would be appropriate, while one rated 10 should be reserved only for those who are very fit, in good walking boots and with all the essential gear for eventualities in the mountains, used to precipitous terrain and, of course, with the stamina for long and strenuous walking. The Cisne climb poses particular risks and these are set out in the notes for that walk (Walk 32).

All the walks are suitable for regular hillwalkers. Nervertheless, hillwalking poses dangers, carries a risk of personal injury, and should be undertaken only by those with a full understanding of the risks, and the training and experience necessary to evaluate them. Neither the author nor the publisher can accept liability for damage of any nature (including personal injury or death, damage to property etc) arising directly or indirectly from information in this book.

THE WALKS

View of Lucero on the return from Los Pradillos (Walk 13)

NERJA AND AROUND

Looking towards Torre de Almendrón (Walk 7)

One of the great advantages of Nerja as a centre for walking is that you can spend a fortnight there and have sufficient choices of walks without the need to hire a car. There are many walks directly from the town, and you can further extend your choices by taking a short bus ride to the white village of Frigiliana. If you end up there and the bus timetable doesn't suit your return to Nerja, it will cost you only €12 for a taxi.

As well as exploring the routes featured in this section, from Nerja you can also:
- Wander up through the Capistrano estate and make the ridge walk to the north. You can walk all day through this wild countryside.
- Walk out of town towards the Cave of Nerja and divert down to Maro, with its spectacular tower.
- Follow along the Río Seco (west of Nerja beyond the Playazo beach), going north to eventually reach Frigiliana, then return via the Río Higuerón.
- Hire a mountain bike and take it to the sierra north of Nerja, which has an endless network of tracks to explore.

Alternatively, you have the option of joining guided walks. Check out Javier's walks (www.andalucianwalks.com) or look up John Keo's website (www.hikingwalkingspain.com). You may be collected from, and dropped back to, Nerja on these tours.

WALK 1
Frigiliana to Nerja via Fuente del Esparto

Start	Plaza del Ingenio, Frigiliana
Finish	The Cave of Nerja
Distance	14km (+2km optional extension to La Presa dam)
Height gain/loss	605m/750m
Difficulty	4
Time	5hr (+30min for optional extension)
Getting there	The most practical way of getting to the start of this walk is to take a bus from Nerja to Frigiliana. Regular buses leave the bus station at the top of the town and, 15min later, arrive at the main square, Plaza del Ingenio, in Frigiliana (///bonanza.venues.saucer).
Options	Diverting off the walk to come back to Nerja via the gorges takes 4km off the distance but adds nearly 1hr to the walk.

This walk would make a good first excursion for getting a feel for the features and landmarks of the Nerja area. It crosses two rivers and skirts under some of the region's high peaks.

Part of the GR 249 *Gran Senda de Málaga*, this route is waymarked, maintained and easy to follow. It is an undulating and rough walk and a little steep in places. The first river crossing is unlikely to cause any difficulty, but the second may be awkward if there has been rain.

The ancient village of **Frigiliana** has a chequered past and was the centre for many industries over its history. Artefacts unearthed here include 3000-year-old Neolithic remains as well as Roman coins. It was a Moorish enclave for centuries and the scene of a bloody battle in 1569.

High up on the mountain of El Fuerte, above the village, there are the remains of two lime kilns, an indication of the old industry that produced mortar and whitewash; the large old building on the

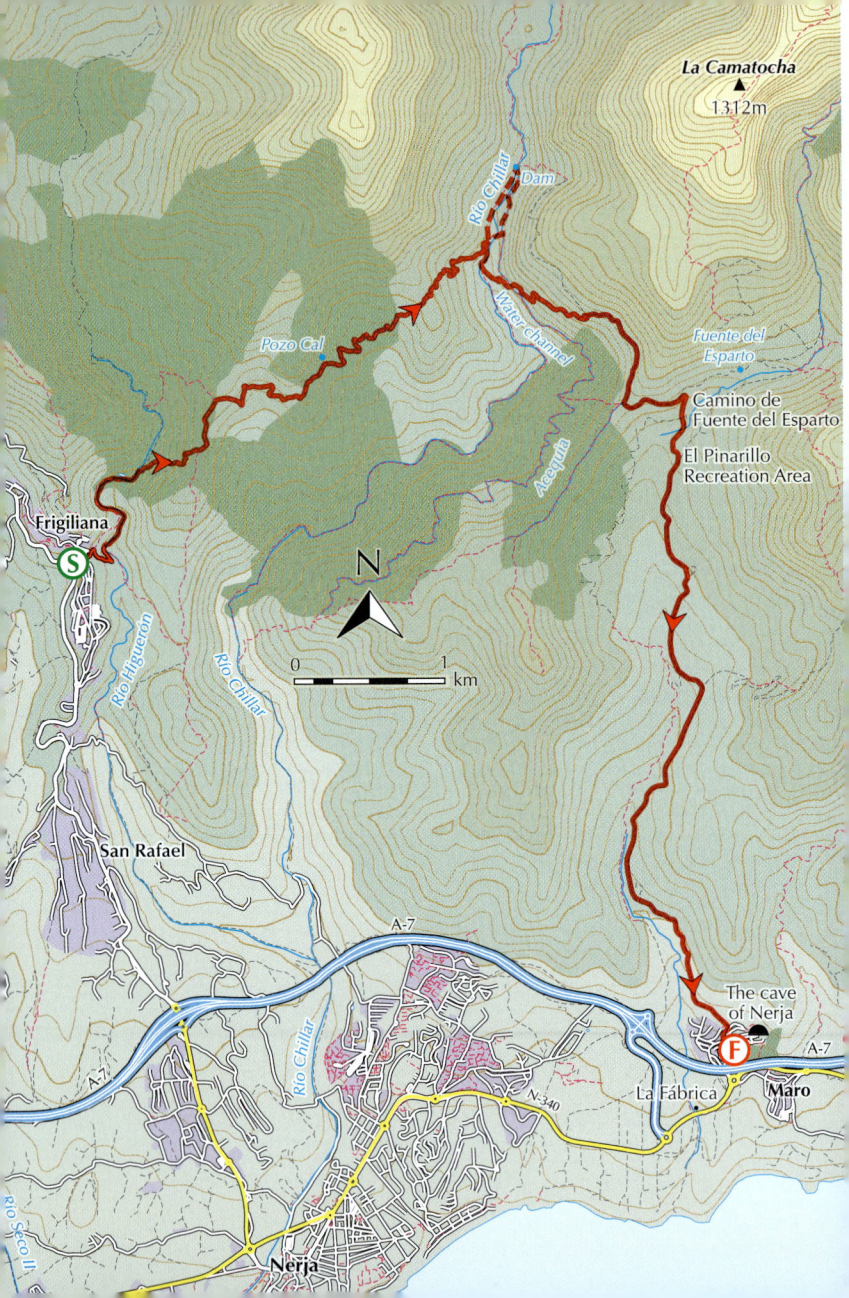

WALK 1 – FRIGILIANA TO NERJA VIA FUENTE DEL ESPARTO

main square, El Ingenio, used to be the sugar factory that existed here from the early 17th century; the tourist office itself, La Casa del Apero (the house of the farm implements) is from the 15th century.

The ceramic plaques of Frigiliana are most interesting and feature in Walk 2.

If you stand in the square facing the obvious tall building, you will see a decorative kiosk in the foreground. Behind the kiosk and off to the left is the stone path up to the centre of the old town. To the right, the stepped path in the opposite direction leads to the tourist office at Casa del Apero. In between these two opposing directions there is an alleyway with signs for the Río Higuerón. This is the route to follow.

The walk descends a steep concrete path down to the riverbed. Going left against the flow of the Río Higuerón, the route passes a reservoir and a grove of gum trees and fenced areas, until it reaches the start of the walk on the right.

From the signpost the trail rises steeply.

Looking up the river valley the high mountain in the distance that has its point flattened at the top is Lucero (1779m). With binoculars you should be able to see the ruins of a building at the top. Immediately to the left of Lucero is its little infant, Lucerillo (the one with the very pointed top). Across the valley from them is the flat plateau of La Cadena (1645m). A careful look shows that there is a sharp two-pronged feature in front of this plateau; this is Cerro Cisne. The mountain that the walk skirts immediately to the left of is Cerro Capriote (1145m).

The waymarkers are rather sparse here – look out for paint marks on nearby rocks if in doubt of the route. The steep path gradually reaches a col from where the trail can be seen off to the right in the distance. The route is now descending to the Río Chillar, with a few ups and downs along the way. It wanders into narrow ravines and out onto open hillside, leading through rosemary, gorse, broom and *esparto* grass, and passing twisted pine trees.

THE MOUNTAINS AROUND NERJA

A third of the way to the Río Chillar, the path reaches a sign for **Pozo Cal**. This means the reservoir of the *calera* (lime kiln). Above the sign are the remnants of what used to be a lime kiln. Limestone was collected and burnt in this kiln, to be crushed into powder for cement and whitewash.

The water channel into Nerja

Long before you reach the river, the sound of the water can be heard as it cascades down over mighty limestone boulders strewn in its path. When you get to the river the trail is not very clear; follow along to the right on the riverbank, until the waymark on the opposite bank can be seen. Do not cross here, however – a few metres further along the bank there is a much safer crossing point. Its location may be marked with small cairns.

▶ The trail rises steeply out of the valley of the Río Chillar and passes over a river channel. This is the main water supply to the town of Nerja.

When you reach the river, you will be at the halfway point.

Extension to the dam at La Presa

The outflow of the river at La Presa, the dam, can be reached by taking the path to the left. This short diversion goes along the side of the channel, precipitous in places, but it provides a flavour of the enormous task that was undertaken in the 1950s to clamp this concrete channel to the sides of the mountains. The round trip to the dam will add half an hour to the walk.

> Three kilometres further above the dam, in the area that is the source of the Río Chillar, you'll come to the ruins of a building, **Cortijo Imán**, the farm of the holy Muslim man, renowned as an area where, in ancient times, tobacco was grown and illicitly marketed. However, at time of publication the track to Cortijo Imán was very overgrown.

An alternative option to the dam is as follows: just before you reach the river there is a path to the left, going upstream. This path will take you to the dam, and you can return along the opposite bank of the river, on top of, or beside, the water channel. Be warned, however, that at time of publication this alternative path to the dam was also quite overgrown.

Main route

Having crossed the river, the path past the water channel is long and steep. It reaches a col and joins a wide,

The aqueduct into La Fábrica

dirt-track road. Turn right along this road and proceed to a wide, open col. Follow the waymarkers at the col and descend to the left until you reach the recreation area of El Pinarillo, but before reaching it the path crosses a wide dirt track. This is the **Camino de Fuente del Esparto** (the path of the fountain of the long grass). A short diversion to the left over this dirt track will take you to the fountain. ◄

The fountain always has fresh water, but you will have to share it with the honey bees that congregate here.

Emerging from **El Pinarillo**, turn right to make the long, gradual descent to the exit from the park and the end of the walk. ◄

Several long kilometres further on, the track emerges onto the road up to the **Cave of Nerja**. From here, public buses into town are infrequent and catching a taxi is only a remote possibility. However, the walk into town along the N-340 is lined with many places of interest.

This dirt track is the elongation of the Camino de Fuente del Esparto and is the track that leads into the start of Walks 6–8 to El Cielo, Almendrón and Navachica.

One feature en route is the area known as **La Fábrica** (the factory). A very famous landmark in the town, it was once a sugar factory and the lands surrounding it were planted with sugar cane. In the early part of the 20th century a distillery was added and a very fine aqueduct was constructed to take water to the factory.

WALK 2
El Fuerte from Frigiliana

Start/Finish	Plaza del Ingenio, Frigiliana; or reservoir car park, Pozo de Lizar
Distance	8.5km
Height gain	670m
Difficulty	4
Time	3hr 30min
Getting there	Regular buses from Nerja stop in the Plaza del Ingenio, the main square in the upper part of the village (///user.sorely.downhill). If arriving by car drive through the village in the direction of Cómpeta and, after 1.5km, take the high road to the right, signposted to the Camino del Fuerte. This will lead to the reservoir where you can park.
Options	Walk back from Frigiliana to Nerja via the Río Higuerón (6km; additional 1hr 30min or 2hr).

El Fuerte, the tough one, rises above and to the northwest of Frigiliana. This walk goes through the stepped, narrow streets of this delightful white village and up the mountain for wonderful views over its tiled roofs to Nerja, down to El Acebuchal and up to the high mountains. The climb follows a well-defined path with lots of opportunities for spotting mountain flowers.

THE MORISCOS' REBELLION

In 1569 a considerable number of Moriscos lived in this area. These were Muslims who had converted to Christianity, and this walk sets off through the *barrio de moriscos*. The Moriscos rebelled against the harsh conditions imposed on them and a Spanish army was dispatched to put down the rebellion. The ensuing conflict moved out of Frigiliana up the mountain. Many Moriscos threw themselves to their deaths off El Fuerte rather than surrender.

THE MOUNTAINS AROUND NERJA

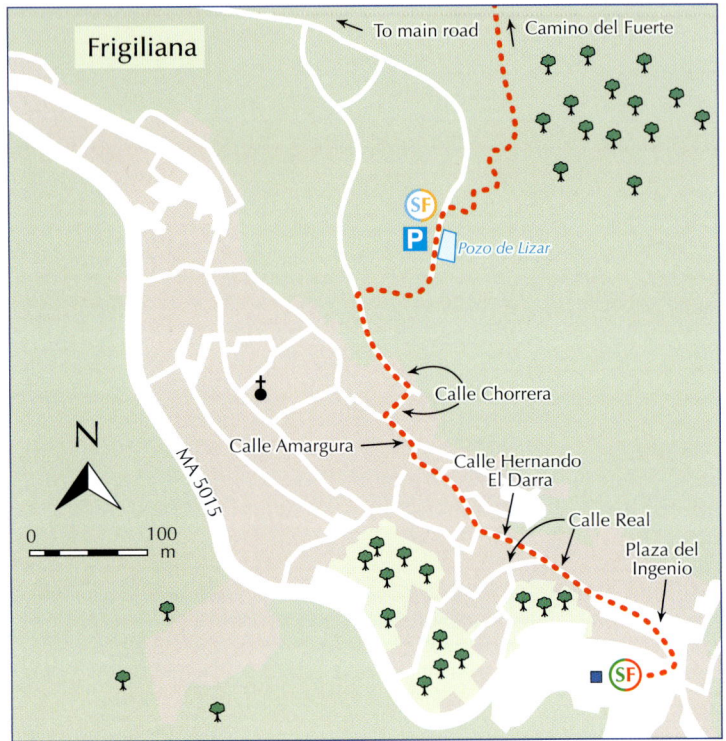

There are no signposts to the Camino del Fuerte from the centre of the village but the locals all know the way, and, should you get lost, the enquiry will be an experience in itself.

◀ The main street leading up through **Frigiliana** from the Plaza del Ingenio is Calle Real. Head up this, always ascending and generally going to the right. (The route follows the ceramic plaques of Frigiliana, which can be examined on your return.)

Taking the first stepped option bear right up Calle Hernando El Darra and carry on into Calle Amargura. Avoiding the turn down Calle Santo Cristo, go left until you reach and carry on into Calle Chorrera. This street will bend to the left and lead you from the cobblestone village street out onto a concrete road into the countryside.

WALK 2 – EL FUERTE FROM FRIGILIANA

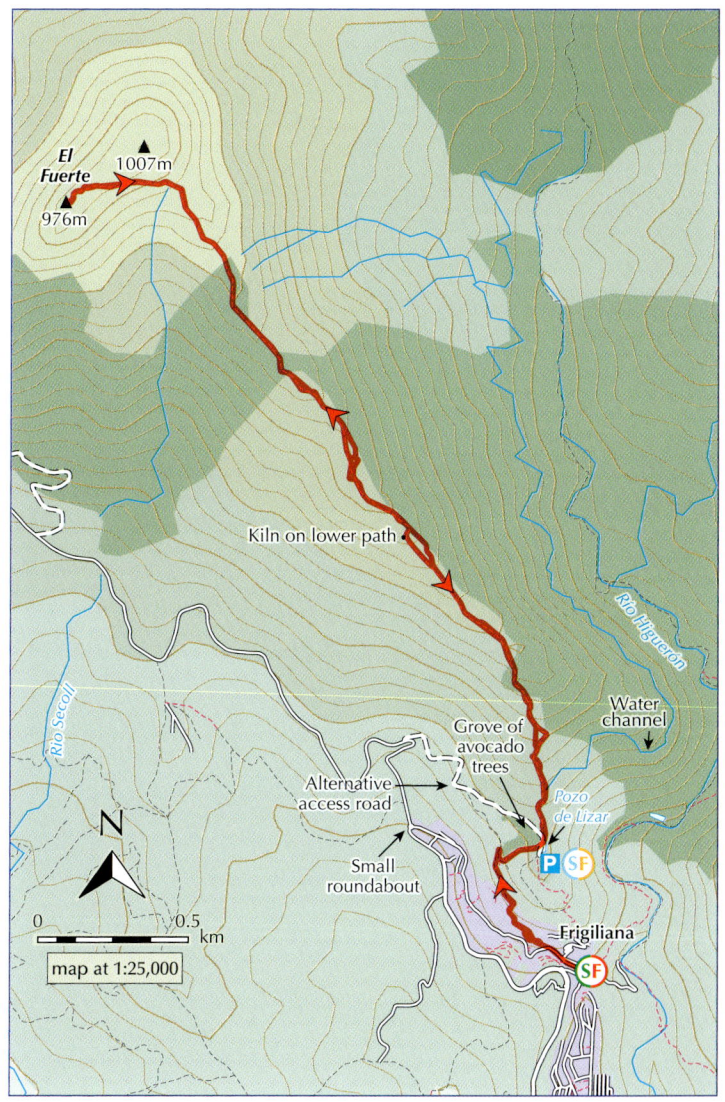

THE MOUNTAINS AROUND NERJA

El Fuerte, viewed from Nerja

After 100m you'll reach a road junction where there is a high retaining wall of conglomerate stone on the right. The route turns sharp right up the steep concrete road until it arrives at a multiple junction. On the right is a pair of brick gateposts. On the left, a rough path skirts around a **grove of avocado trees**. This is the path to the reservoir.

Take this path as it narrows and eventually emerges onto a road where you can hear the sound of the water from the channel discharging into the reservoir. This area is known as **Pozo de Lizar** (*pozo* means well).

Turn left and follow the water channel to pass the first waymark on your right. This is the start of the Camino del Fuerte.

The walk follows a waymarked, stepped path that is steepest at the start and gradually develops into a gentler gradient.

> The **solid limestone** is vertically bedded with a slight dip to the west and the distinct bedding planes in it can be seen. This limestone will contrast with the weathered limestone further up.

WALK 2 – EL FUERTE FROM FRIGILIANA

The path meanders through pine woodland and is bordered by rosemary and broom bushes.

No matter what time of year, there is always an abundance of **wildflowers** on El Fuerte. The low-lying kidney vetch (*vulneraria* in Spanish) may be seen at the sides of the path and blooms in the springtime, while the fringed pink (*clavelina* in Spanish) is an autumn flower. Worth looking out for is the *cistus*, or rock rose (*flor de jara* in Spanish), which is plentiful thanks to the mountain's lime-rich soil.

The well-trodden path passes the remains of a bee-hive stone structure on the right and at this point you are halfway to the summit.

This stone structure is in fact the ruin of a **lime kiln**. Limestone was collected on the mountain and burnt in such kilns to reduce it to a powder. The powder was then used as a mortar for construction and as whitewash to paint the houses.

(If you miss the kiln on the way up due to the fallen trees from 2020 that now have to be bypassed, you may see it on the descent, noting that, where there is a choice of paths you should take the lower option.) The summit is marked by a metal sign and a triangulation point. However, it is not the highest point of the mountain. The triangulation point is at 976m, but the highest point, 500m to the north, is at 1007m. There is no path to it and to get there is a scramble through inhospitable terrain.

> Below the triangulation point to the west is the village of **El Acebuchal**. It is from this spot that the Moriscos plunged to their deaths in 1569. To the north the high cone-shaped peak of Lucero (1779m) dominates; across the valley the flat-topped mountain is La Cadena. Off to the south the view is over Frigiliana and down to Nerja.

There is no other option but to return on the same path to Frigiliana. On the return you can see that Frigiliana is divided into two parts. The older part is nearest El Fuerte and the newer extension is furthest away. As the path approaches the base, you can see the river channel that carries water to the reservoir. This water has come from a dam on the Río Higuerón.

> As you descend through the village it is worth examining some of the **ceramic plaques** on the walls. These were erected in the 1960s and tell the history of the village. Plaque No 3, at the bottom of Calle Amargura and the top of Calle Hernando El Darra reads:
> 'Andrés el Chorairán, native *monfí* from Sedella, encouraged the spirits of his people to bring them to rebellion. The young people who started to agitate were refrained by the Moor, Luis Méndez, an influential man in Canillas, but he couldn't stop them attacking the inn of a Christian and killing several people in it. The judge of Vélez, Pedro Guerra, came along and many innocent Moors,

WALK 2 – EL FUERTE FROM FRIGILIANA

Ceramic plaque in Frigiliana

among them, Luis Méndez, who had stopped the revolt, were imprisoned and burdened with chains, and subjected to cruel torture.'

The main street of the Calle Real winds its way past the town hall to the church.

Part of the **Iglesia San Antonio de Padua** dates as far back as the period of the Morisco rebellion. It is a quaint old church and well worth a visit. In front of the church there is a square with a restaurant.

Extension to Nerja

Walking back to Nerja will take from 1½ to 2 hours. It can be done via the gorge of the Río Higuerón (see Walk 4). Alternatively, you can return by road and take the obvious detour before a small restaurant above the Higuerón riverbed.

The Mountains around Nerja

WALK 3
El Fuerte from El Acebuchal

Start/Finish	El Acebuchal
Distance	8km
Height gain	510m
Difficulty	7
Time	4hr 30min
Getting there	2.5km beyond Frigiliana take the turning to the right signposted El Acebuchal. This rough, narrow road turns into a dirt track and reaches El Acebuchal over 2km into the mountains. Park at the entrance to the riverbed, at a sharp left-hand bend just short of El Acebuchal (///length.ogle.defeats).
Options	If you can, arrange a lift to El Acebuchal, climb to the summit and descend to Frigiliana, thus avoiding the walk's difficult descent back to the start point.
Warning	The descent route is a narrow ill-defined path through thick vegetation; follow the cairns and markers.

Offering the opportunity to explore the 'Lost Village of El Acebuchal', this walk is not for the fainthearted, with a short, taxing climb and difficult descent for those who like a challenge. The climb has a degree of scrambling. But the greatest difficulty is on the way down (see Warning, above). You should get to the summit in an hour and a half but will need double that time for the descent. Wearing shorts is not recommended.

Like many places in the mountains around Nerja, the tiny village of **El Acebuchal** was frequented by the Maquis, Republicans who resisted Franco. In the summer of 1949 the Guardia Civil ordered that El Acebuchal be cleared of its 200 inhabitants, and a military garrison took up residence. The abandoned mountain hamlet soon fell into disrepair and eventually into ruins, becoming known locally as the 'Lost Village' or *Pueblo de los Fantasmas* – Village of Ghosts.

WALK 3 – EL FUERTE FROM EL ACEBUCHAL

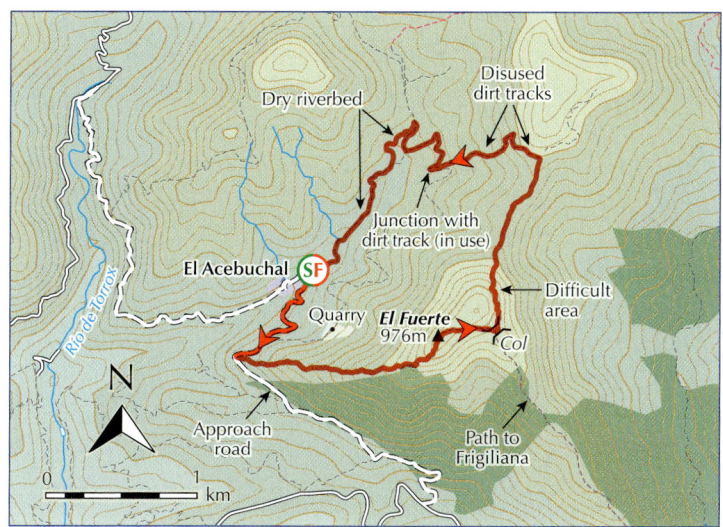

Fifty years later in 1998, Antonio García Sánchez, son of one of the original villagers, returned with his wife, Virtudes, and family to restore a house in the village. Once this was completed, they rebuilt a further five houses and the tavern. Other former residents returned to their old family homes to begin their restoration, so that today, all 36 houses, the chapel, tavern and cobblestone streets have been returned to how they once were.

Walk back up the road for 1km, passing a dirt track on your left (leading into a disused quarry). One hundred metres beyond the **quarry-road junction**, at a sharp bend in the road to the left, climb up to the left off the dirt track.

The path is up through a pine forest and is reasonably well defined. As you approach the summit of **El Fuerte** there are one or two precipitous sections and some scrambling. Walk over bare rock to the summit.

Scrambling up El Fuerte

Before you embark on the descent heed the warning above. Follow the GPX if you managed to download it onto a mobile or GPS.

◄ Descend from the summit down a steep path, northeast, in the opposite direction to the ascent. After half an hour or so you will reach a **col**. From this col head left and north, off the main path. Watch out for a cairn at this col (the main path goes to Frigiliana). The narrow path leads off to the left, going close to the base of an overhanging cliff. Be extra careful when passing ravines where the scree may give way. The path winds its way to and over a rough ridge, thence to a **disused dirt track**.

Follow the disused dirt track to meet another dirt track leading down to the left. This second track leads to a **used dirt track**, at a bend. Turn right here and descend to a junction, where there is a dried-up riverbed on the left. Descend into the riverbed and follow it for several kilometres back to **El Acebuchal**.

WALK 4
La Cruz del Pinto

Start/Finish	Calle Puente Viejo, Nerja
Distance	8km
Height gain	370m
Difficulty	2
Time	4hr 30min (3hr 30min by the high-level return route)
Getting there	Head for the car park at the end of Calle Puente Viejo (///curled.fattier.prototypes), the street just off the first roundabout at the (lower) entrance to the town (beyond Parque Verano Azul).

This short climb to the nearest high viewpoint above Nerja returns along the gorge of the Río Higuerón. Depending on the time of year, be prepared to get your feet wet in the river on the way back.

Walk out of Nerja along the **Río Chillar** under the motorway and up past the cement factory. Immediately after the cement factory, and before the quarry, there is a culvert over the river beside a tall gum tree. The walk crosses over this culvert to climb the concrete road and proceed between houses, ignoring all minor paths off it. The route contours around the mountain to climb it from the southwest.

At a crossroads there is a steep path down to the left and a rough gravel road up to the right, before the gates of, and running alongside, No 61. Walk up this road. ▸

Stay on the rough gravel road, passing all houses, to head out into the country. The road comes to a point where there is a Y intersection, with two concrete roads stretching off ahead. Take the road on the right that goes up to Quinto Pino.

If you miss the turning, further along there is a dead-end lane and sign on the left, at No 19; turn right just after this along a rough gravel path to rejoin the walk, following a sign for a house called Quinto Pino.

The Mountains around Nerja

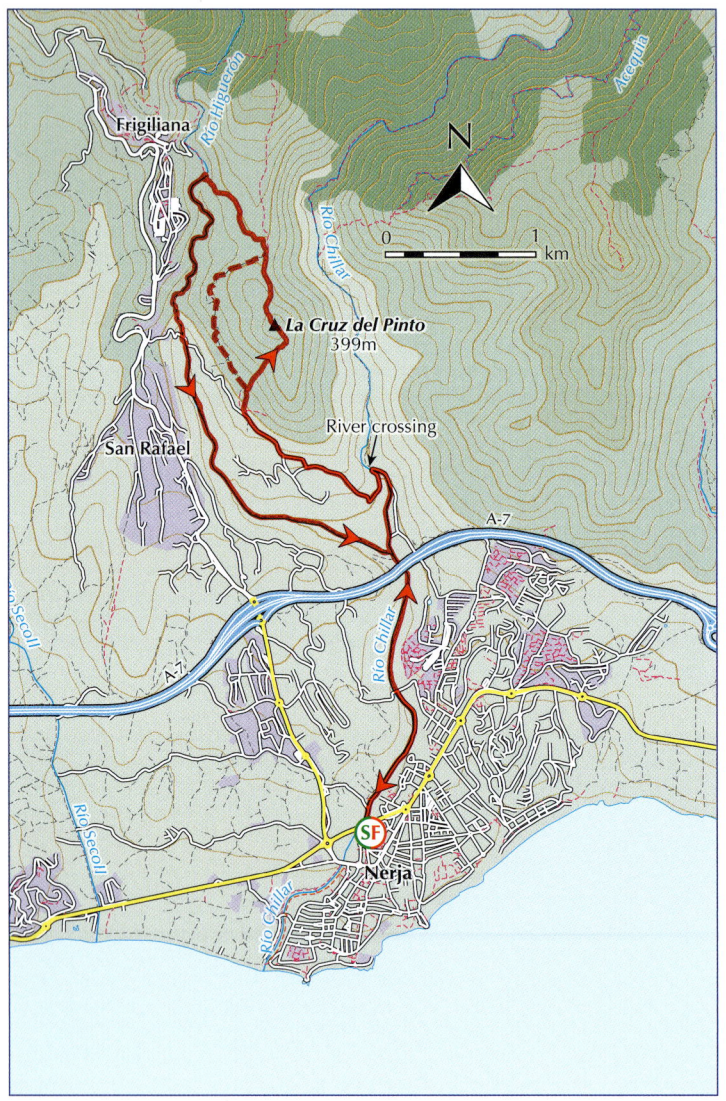

WALK 4 – LA CRUZ DEL PINTO

The summit of La Cruz del Pinto

THE STORY OF LA CRUZ DEL PINTO

Francisco Pinto was a sea captain whose ship was in danger of sinking during a wild storm in the Mediterranean. Pinto went on his knees and gave a solemn undertaking that, if he and his crew were saved, he would erect a cross on the nearest mountain to where he came ashore. He managed to drop anchor at Burriana Beach and soon afterwards erected the cross on this mountain. (Some would say that he cheated and that his cross should have been erected on El Cielo, a far more formidable task.)

Walk up the concrete road for a short distance until the road turns to the left and descends to the gates of Quinto Pino (a private house). There are signs on the right – one of them, a Parque Natural sign, is on the side of a track that has cairns on either side of it. ▶ This track winds its way to the summit, a mere 20 minutes away.

This is where the shorter version of the route returns.

49

There are a few steep steps over bare rock on the approach to the summit of **La Cruz del Pinto** (399m) where you'll find a cross set into a concrete block. ◄ From the summit there are fine views over Nerja and the coast, west to Frigiliana and north to the Almijaras.

> Within the cross there is a tabernacle, which contains religious objects.

On the north side of the summit, find the path going down towards Frigiliana. The track is a little steep in places. Eventually it arrives at a clearing where there are multiple paths. Take the path going down to the Río Higuerón.

Shorter high-level return route
The road on the immediate left at this junction is the shorter return option that hugs the side of the mountain. To follow this route, keep left at all junctions. The road passes above the Quinto Pino house, where it rejoins the outward route.

Main route
The walk back via the **Río Higuerón** is much more interesting than the flat return at high level. You will need to wade through the river, where water may be ankle deep, but the experience is well worth it. ◄ The path meanders from the left riverbank to the river itself and out to the right bank. In the river are enormous limestone boulders, the largest of which have steps around them.

> There is a gorge en route that is similar to the Chillar gorge, although not as spectacular.

Emerge eventually onto the gravel river plain and walk on the dirt track back to **Nerja**.

WALK 5
The Gorges of the Río Chillar

Start/Finish	Calle Puente Viejo, Nerja
Alternative Start/Finish	About 1km further up the riverbank, if passable
Distance	15km (13km from the alternative start point)
Height gain	340m
Difficulty	3
Time	4hr (3hr 30min from the alternative start point)
Getting there	Head for the car park (///pirated.relents.vocalists) at the end of Calle Puente Viejo, the street just off the first roundabout at the (lower) entrance to the town (beyond Parque Verano Azul). Alternatively, drive up through town, turn down Calle Picasso and turn right at the end of the road to find somewhere to park.
Options	You can climb higher up to the dam at La Presa or up to the top of the ravine to walk its ridge, or just visit the gorge if you don't have time for the climb.
Note	This walk should not be done on a day when heavy rainfall is forecast. The water can rise suddenly after rain. Shorts are essential and some walkers go in swimsuits. Bring a towel if you want to take a dip.

If there is one walk that every visitor to Nerja should do, then it's this one. After the Cave of Nerja the gorges are the second biggest tourist attraction here. You can touch the sides of these cliffs with each hand and yet they are so tall that the sky is shut out. During the summer they are crammed with people escaping the heat of the coast in the cool waters.

The route described here goes in the opposite direction to the route that most people follow, climbing up first to circle over the gorges and then descending to walk out along the river. This way your feet stay dry until the final stages and your legs don't get as wet when you are walking with, rather than against, the river's flow.

WALK 5 – THE GORGES OF THE RÍO CHILLAR

There are many access points to the river, the most obvious being from the car park at the end of Calle Puente Viejo and another to park along the riverbank near Calle Picasso, subject to the state of the riverbank and road.

Walk along the bank of the **Río Chillar**. You will pass a seven-storey block of flats on Calle Picasso that is built on top of the rock, with a cave underneath. As the road passes under the **motorway** you can also spot a white house perched high above, immediately under the carriageway. The front wall of the house hides a cave in the rock. Tall bamboos line the route at this point; later on, groves of avocados do so.

The walk passes a former quarry where pink limestone was once extracted. From here you need to pick your way along the river, crossing it many times on the stone dams, trying to stay dry. Two and a half kilometres beyond the motorway is the **electricity generating station**. The path turns off to the right 50m before you get to it. On the right, some 30m beyond a circular red-bricked structure in the river (and 50m short of the concrete ramp up to the generating station), the route begins to climb up a gravel scree slope. The start of this route has been obliterated by construction work during the maintenance of the water channel. Above the scree slope the water channel has a cover and the path comes off this cover.

The path is steep and narrow. It joins concrete steps and rises again. For a section the walk follows alongside a large-diameter pipe, then it rises to a reservoir on the higher river channel. At the upper reservoir, or further along the water channel (see Detour, below), there is the option to climb up to the top of the ravine. Now it follows the concrete river channel as it contours around the side of the ravine.

> This **water channel** (*acequia*) is the water supply to Nerja. It comes from the dam higher up the river, generates electricity at the station and flows into the town. The channel is very popular with toads, which dive in and look up from the base.

The water channel goes through a high cave, *Cueva de las Palomas* (Cave of the Doves).

Detour to the top of the ravine
About 100m before the cave there is a cairn and a path that leads up to the crest of the ravine. This option is well worth the effort but, if you lack the energy at this point, continue along the water channel. The higher path is narrow and goes through encroaching vegetation, but the views are better and you don't need to watch every step (which you do if you opt for the water channel).

Main route
The channel eventually arrives at a point where a path crosses it. Here, descend into the river, turn left to head for the gorges and then retrace your outward route back towards **Nerja**. ◄

Some walkers bring sandals to wade through the water, but others keep the ankle support and just get their boots and socks wet. There are many deep pools for a quick dip.

The **gorges**, or *los cahorros*, are in a series of three narrow passageways cut deep through the rock. The Spanish word *chillar* means to scream, and you can imagine how the water screams through these narrow chasms in flood conditions.

When you reach the **electricity station** it's easy to spot the water supply channel clinging to the ravine. Follow the Río Chillar back to the start of the walk.

Through the Río Chillar gorges

WALK 6
El Cielo circuit

Start/Finish	Road junction, 4km along the Pinarillo track
Distance	14km
Height gain	1180m
Difficulty	8
Time	7hr
Getting there	From Nerja, follow signs to La Cueva de Nerja, and then turn northwards up the Pinarillo track, a dirt-track road that goes off to the left immediately before the car park for the cave. Park at the first major junction (///mutiny.mafias.footballers), a fork in the road with a sign offering choices of a recreation area to the left and a *sendero* (path) to the right.
Options	If you have two cars leave one of them 1km past the recreation area and take 2km of road-walking off the route.
Note	The Pinarillo track is closed to cars during the summer, usually June to September (check before you set off), which would add a further 8km to the walk (but see Walk 23 as an alternative). The early part of the walk is through vegetation that may be dense.

This is one of the really great walks of the Almijaras. El Cielo (1508m), from which you can see the mountains of Navachica, Almendrón, Lucero and La Maroma, is only 8km from Nerja and it looms majestically over the town. This walk is also an excellent introduction to many of the landmarks in the Almijaras: it follows the Pinarillo track, where many walks start, and visits the Barranco de los Cazadores. You're certain to spot those other local features – the *cabra montés* – too.

Set off north towards El Pinarillo recreation area. Water bottles can be topped up here and there's a wooded picnic spot along the path. The walk direction initially is towards **Fuente del Esparto**.

THE MOUNTAINS AROUND NERJA

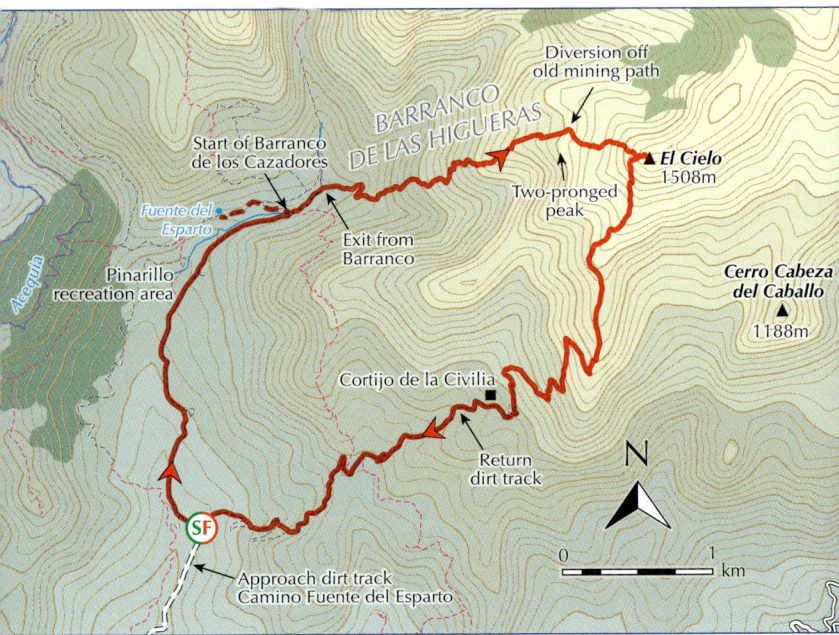

The **Fuente del Esparto** is a well-known landmark in the area and it is worth a little diversion to see it. A kilometre beyond the recreation area the road takes a sharp left where it crosses the Barranco de los Cazadores (the ravine of the hunters). The fountain is 500m up the road away from the ravine.

The route enters the ravine and passes over a dry riverbed. Shortly, some 50m past a cave, there is a set of cairns and a narrow, rather ill-defined path on the right that leads into the **Barranco de las Higueras**. The path is tight and it is necessary to squeeze between rosemary, spiky furze and the occasional broom. **Do not** proceed into the depths of Barranco de las Higueras, but divert to the right – there is no other path. It is extremely important to make sure that you are on the path here.

WALK 6 – EL CIELO CIRCUIT

The path is narrow and quite steep, but it widens as it ascends. This is an old mining trail, its destination a disused mine on the side of El Cielo. The path eventually flattens as it approaches a **two-pronged peak** jutting up from the mountain. It is important to be careful here, for the **old mining path** begins to descend but the circuit leaves it, turning right.

From here to the summit the route is defined by little cairns. In this sparse vegetation the cairns at times compete for attention and on occasions are absent. However, the route is upwards towards the summit cross, which should now be visible.

Eventually a short rock scramble is required to reach the summit of **El Cielo** (1508m).

Giant asphodels at the foot of El Cielo

When it was first erected, the galvanised **summit cross** had a full mirror on the side facing Nerja. The intention was that the sun would shine on it and reflect down into the town. It did just that, but, because it was erected upright, the intended effect only occurred during a few days in winter. Over time the mirror got broken and was replaced in 2012.

From the summit you can see that El Cielo is not an isolated peak, but rather the shoulder of a mountain ridge that stretches up to Navachica. Down from Navachica on the other shoulder is Cerro Cisne, and in the middle, under Navachica, is Almendrón. Beyond Almendrón in the distance is the hump of La Maroma.

The descent is on the same side of the mountain as the ascent. If there are other climbers there it is most likely they came up from the southwest. This is your way down, via a cleft in the mountain with slippery scree that requires care. The direction is initially towards the west (almost in the direction of ascent), but the well-defined path swings to the south and is waymarked. After about half an hour, the gradient becomes far gentler than the ascent, and the route circles another pair of peaks jutting from the mountain before reaching some zig-zags. You emerge from these by a collection of ruins of old and modern buildings. This is **Cortijo de la Civilia**. ◂

> Apparently, an eccentric woman once lived here, going around in the clothes of a policeman.

From the *cortijo* (country farmhouse) the path becomes a dirt track. A few kilometres further down, the road begins to zig-zag and it is possible to take shortcuts on a narrower path until you finally reach your parking place at the road junction.

Virtually the whole mountain of El Cielo is a **blue-grey limestone**. It is in massive formation and unweathered, in contrast to the rock on, say El Fuerte, which is white and friable. Along the approaches to El Cielo the route passes outcrops of limestone conglomerate.

WALK 7
The tour of Almendrón

Start/Finish	El Pinarillo recreation area
Alternative Start/Finish	Entrance to the Barranco de los Cazadores, 1km beyond the recreation area
Distance	12km from Pinarillo (10km from entrance to Barranco de los Cazadores)
Height gain	930m
Difficulty	9
Time	6hr from Pinarillo
Getting there	From Nerja, follow signs to La Cueva de Nerja, and then turn northwards up the Pinarillo track, a dirt-track road that goes off to the left immediately before the car park for the cave. Follow this for 5km to the recreation area (///operative.disordered.countryside). Park here or, if your car is up to it, continue 1km on the track to the entrance to Barranco de los Cazadores.
Options	The Pinarillo track is closed to cars during the summer, usually June to September (check before you set off), which would add a further 11km to the walk. If you wish to explore the bat cave, bring a torch. A short detour can be made to the top of Tajo del Sol (1550m). You could do this walk in reverse and rise to Almendrón sooner.

Almendrón is the jagged peak that can be seen from Nerja. It is said that Almendrón has many faces and, indeed, the views from Frigiliana and from Cómpeta are starkly different. The mountain is named after the natural limestone feature on its flank – an almond (*almendro*)-shaped tower – that cannot be seen from the town. This walk does not climb to any summit but merely passes under its stark features through some of the most breathtaking mountain scenery in the Almijaras.

This is not a waymarked walk but it follows a well-worn path. The difficulty rating is high because it is arduous in places, requires careful manoeuvring over boulders and scree, and involves a little scrambling. The walk can be divided into four parts: two hours in the ravine until the turn is made up and out of it; one hour to the highest point of the walk; a further hour to make the traverse and have lunch; and another hour to descend.

WALK 7 – THE TOUR OF ALMENDRÓN

Walk up the dirt track heading northeast from **El Pinarillo recreation area** towards Fuente del Esparto. After 1.5km the road turns sharp left over the ravine and the official route to Almendrón begins. There is a **pumphouse** and many gum trees here. Turn right off the road (continuing northeast) and into the Barranco de los Cazadores (ravine of the hunters).

> Within this quiet and sheltered canyon **plants** such as the Andalucían thistle flourish. The delicate cade juniper (or prickly juniper) tree is also here, with its profusion of red/brown berries in spring and summer.

The walk into the ravine passes caves and meets a track on the left that also leads up to Fuente del Esparto. Further along there is an old lime kiln.

> The ravine was once a significant **watercourse** and it is clear to see how rapid waters eroded the rock. There are many boulders, brought down by flood waters, that fill the canyon in places.

The path reaches a point where there has been a major rock slippage on the left and small cairns invite the walker to exit the base of the ravine, reaching an old mining trail that follows high on the wall of the ravine.

Eventually you reach the area of the mines. To get to the bat cave, descend into the base of the ravine and circle back, reaching an enormous boulder. To the left and behind the boulder is the **bat cave**, which was used in the past for mining lead. The bats (*murciélagos* in Spanish) hang from the roof of the cave, so close that you could nearly lift them off. They are nothing to be scared of, so long as you don't disturb them.

The route soon turns back onto the former riverbed, and about 1km along you'll reach the critical turn. There is a large cairn in the bed of the ravine and another cairn on the left. Markings on the rocks point straight on to the path to Navachica and left to Almendrón.

On the mining trail through Barranco de los Cazadores

There follows an hour of strenuous climbing, with Tajo del Sol (1550m) on the right. Near the top there are multiple paths, but any of those going southwest will pass under Almendrón.

ALMENDRÓN

The complex of Almendrón has five main features:

- Tajo del Sol (1550m)
- Tajo de Almendrón (1515m)
- La Puerta – a gate/door in the ridge that connects Tajo de Almendrón to Torre de Almendrón
- Torre de Almendrón – the almond-shaped tower
- La Camatocha (1312m) – the beginning of the descent

Extension to Tajo del Sol

On the approach to the col there is the option of taking the path to the right, which goes to the top of **Tajo del Sol** (cliff of the sun). It is a one-hour diversion that is well worth the extra effort. Beyond Tajo del Sol, the path continues to climb Navachica (Walk 8).

WALK 7 – THE TOUR OF ALMENDRÓN

Main route

One of the main reasons why this walk has been given a difficulty rating of 9 is now before us. Perhaps lunch should be postponed until the safety of the high ground beyond Torre de Almendrón has been reached. Care is required when making the traverse under the cliffs of Almendrón, especially negotiating firstly the boulder scree, then the stone scree. The path can be ill-defined in places. Taking lower routes is recommended. The energetic can deviate off the path and climb to the top of **Tajo de Almendrón**, but there is no clear track to it.

At the southwestern extremity of the traverse, past **Torre de Almendrón**, there is a crest that is the start of the descent. At this crest a climb up to **La Camatocha** will be rewarded with stunning views over the reverse side of the ridge and down the sheer drop into the Barranco de Almendrón.

The path down off La Camatocha is through rosemary and gorse that becomes more and more intrusive. The path passes through a gully at the base of a gorge. ▶

In the springtime miniature daffodils bloom here.

After half an hour or more the path emerges onto the end of a dirt track. You could turn left and follow this track all the way home but it is shorter to go right and descend along a narrow track, thus bypassing the lower road and emerging onto the same dirt track further down.

Next you have the option to turn left to descend into the **Barranco de los Cazadores** and then turn right to return to the starting point. Alternatively, you can turn right and wander up to **El Fuente del Esparto**, which is worth a visit. ▶

There are lots of beehives around here and the bees tend to congregate around the fountain; be careful, they can be aggressive if disturbed.

THE MOUNTAINS AROUND NERJA

WALK 8
Navachica

Start/Finish	Barranco de los Cazadores (preferred)/El Pinarillo recreation area
Distance	15km (16km via Tajo del Sol/Almendrón)
Height gain	1485m
Difficulty	7
Time	8hr (9hr via Tajo del Sol/Almendrón)
Getting there	From Nerja follow the signs to La Cueva de Nerja and then turn left and northwards, just before the parking area for the cave on the dirt-track road to El Pinarillo recreation area. Park here, or preferably drive on for another 1km until the track turns sharp left (///unbreakable.datable.presently). This is the entrance to the Barranco de los Cazadores (the ravine of the hunters). Park here and walk into the *barranco*.
Options	Before embarking on this walk, check to make sure the barrier at the Cave of Nerja is open. It is usually closed from June through to September, but, if there has been a very dry summer, it may remain closed during October. If the barrier is closed it will extend the walk by 11km. Getting to the summit of Navachica may be quite sufficient for most people as a one-day expedition. However, for the adventurous, there is the option of descending via Tajo del Sol and Almendrón (see Walk 7). The descent is precipitous and requires very careful attention to cairns and markers. It involves scrambling down a sheer cliff face.

Navachica is the second highest mountain in the area covered by this book. At 1832m it dominates the eastern end of the mountains of Nerja, vying with La Maroma in the west. With the exception of Lopera, it is the nearest of these mountains to the Sierra Nevada, where, on a spring morning, you get the best view of snow-capped Mulhacén.

WALK 8 – NAVACHICA

Start at the entrance to the **Barranco de los Cazadores**, proceeding into the *barranco* (ravine) and following it northeastwards. The route leads all the way through this ravine up to its end. Become acquainted with the cairns and paint marks that guide you along the path. After

Lunch on the summit of Navachica

2–3km the marks direct you out of the barranco, climbing steeply to join an old mining trail. This well-preserved path passes several mines, the first on the left and the last at the end of a descent.

If you turn to the right into the valley at the last of the **mines** and walk back you will find a cave on the left near a large boulder. This **cave** (a former mine) is now home to a small colony of bats (see Walk 7). ◀

The bats sleep during the day, so your intrusion will not affect them. You will need a torch to enter the cave.

The trail continues and returns to the barranco eventually passing the exit on the left to Almendrón. Cairns and marks on the rocks indicate the alternative routes to Almendrón and Navachica (the latter heads straight on through the barranco). After several kilometres the trail rises steeply, first over bare limestone then through stony inclines. There is a critical turn to the right – it should be quite clear from the markers, but it is important not to miss it, for to proceed straight would take you over very steep ground. In under a kilometre, the trail reaches the Navachica ridge, where there is a welcome rest area. Next turn left towards the summit.

The trail continues and returns to the barranco eventually passing the exit on the left to Almendrón. Cairns and marks on the rocks indicate the alternative routes to Almendrón and Navachica (the latter heads straight on through the barranco). After several kilometres the trail rises steeply, first over bare limestone then through stony inclines. There is a critical turn to the right – it should be quite clear from the markers, but it is important not to miss it, for to proceed straight would take you over very steep ground. In under another kilometre, further the trail reaches the Navachica ridge, where there is a welcome rest area. Next turn left towards the summit.

The approach to the summit of **Navachica** is over bare rock where the markers are not easy to see, so take care to remember the way back.

> From the **summit of Navachica**, marked by a concrete plinth, you will be rewarded with the clearest view (from the mountains of Nerja) of the snow-capped Sierra Nevada. It is also possible to see the two ridges that project out like arms from Navachica, one over to Almendrón and the other towards El Cielo. The double hump of Cerro Cisne, not visible from Nerja or many other places, can also be seen clearly from here.

The safest route back is to return by the ascent route, taking care on the sections of steep, stony paths.

Optional descent via Tajo del Sol and Almendrón

There is no distinct path from Navachica over to Almendrón, ▶ so it is necessary to find a way to descend down and along the ridge. On the approach to Tajo del Sol cairns mark the only viable path, and it is essential to find these cairns. Next the trail descends the cliff face of Tajo del Sol, zig-zagging its way down. When it reaches level ground there are a few kilometres of walking until the route reaches the paths of Almendrón.

There are two choices here: proceed straight under Almendrón or turn left. If you intend to walk over and under Almendrón, it would be wise to read the advice in Walk 7. This option involves some scrambling over scree and boulders to pass by Torre de Almendrón, the rock that is shaped like an almond.

The shorter option is to turn left upon meeting the Almendrón paths and descend back into the barranco.

This alternative descent is reserved for the adventurous, and requires good navigation skills and great care over bare rock.

THE CÓMPETA AREA

The white mountain village of Cómpeta, with La Maroma in the background

Cómpeta is another of Andalucía's delightful white mountain villages. Clamped to the hillside, it is deep into the Almijaras and nestles under La Maroma. The town is 10 minutes down the motorway from Nerja followed by 20 minutes of hairpin bends. Not a village that is vehicle-friendly, its narrow, steep streets wind up the hillside.

There are numerous walking opportunities from the village so you will see other walkers with their boots and sticks. What is featured here is only a selection of the many walks in and around Cómpeta.

The first three of the walks can be combined to make longer walks. From La Fábrica de la Luz, Walk 9 goes to Puerto Blanquillo; the following two walks, to Lucero and to Cerro de la Chapa, start from Puerto Blanquillo.

WALK 9
La Fábrica de la Luz

Start/Finish	Car park at La Fábrica de la Luz
Distance	13km
Height gain	530m
Difficulty	2
Time	4hr
Getting there	Take the motorway and exit to Cómpeta, winding up the many hairpins to the village. Do not enter the village but bypass it in the direction of Canillas de Albaida. This is a mere 2km further on. On the approach to Canillas watch out for the sign – before you enter the village – to the recreation area of La Fábrica de la Luz and follow this peaceful country road for 3.5km to the car park (///riotous.culminates.times).
Options	The walk can be combined with Walk 10 to Lucero or Walk 11 to La Chapa.

This is a gentle circular walk along a river in a sheltered ravine through varied countryside, returning via a dirt track along the rim of the ravine. The route used to be waymarked, but the waymarkers were removed in 2022. Nevertheless, the path and route are quite clear and well trodden.

La Fábrica de la Luz (the factory of light) is 3.5km from Canillas de Albaida. It is a collection of old buildings – until the 1950s a hydroelectric generating station – from where several walks start. There is a designated place for camping, and it is a popular spot for people to come and picnic on a Sunday.

At the parking area there is a dirt track on the right. This will be the return route. ▶ Walk 9 sets off in the direction you have driven in, down as far as the river, turning right just short of the river. You will follow this river, criss-crossing it many times, all the way to Puerto Blanquillo,

It is a new, waymarked path leading up to Puerto Blanquillo and beyond it to Puerto de Cómpeta, a linear walk, with not a lot of interest.

THE MOUNTAINS AROUND NERJA

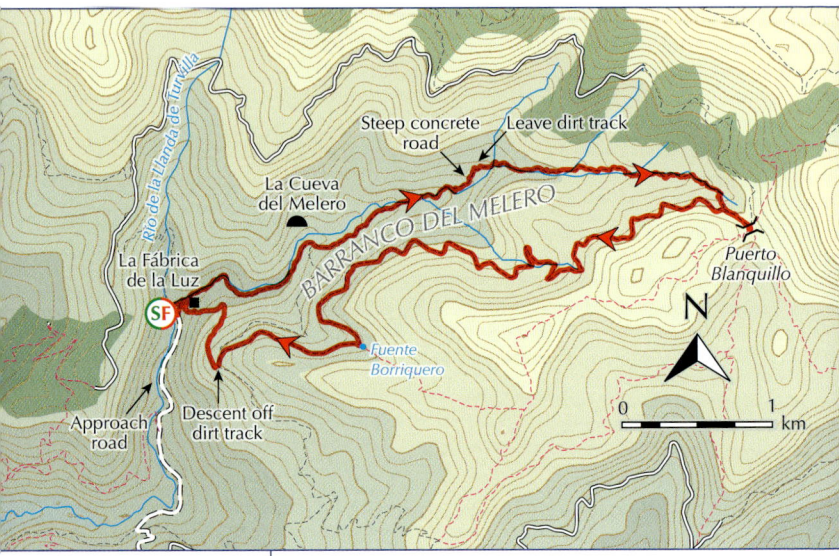

At one of the cortijos there is a grove of Spanish chestnut trees; the chestnuts are harvested in the autumn and brought down by mule.

Walks 10 and 11 to Lucero and La Chapa reach their start points via this approach track.

although the river becomes non-existent further up the ravine. On the way the route passes a large cave, **Cueva del Melero** (cave of the beekeeper; nowadays the cave is a shelter for farm animals), from which the ravine, **Barranco del Melero**, takes its name. It also passes three farmhouses (*cortijos*), Cortijo del Melero, Cortijo de Moreno and Cortijo de Camacho. ◄

After climbing a steep, concrete section of road, be careful to follow the cairns and leave the dirt track, taking the narrower path to the right. The path winds its way through a valley to rise up to a wide, white dirt-track road. ◄ Turning right on this dirt track will take you back towards La Fábrica de la Luz. But first turn left to go 500m up to **Puerto Blanquillo**.

> **Puerto Blanquillo** is a col at an elevation of 1208m. The road passing over it eventually arrives back on the other side of Canillas de Albaida. Looking over

WALK 9 – LA FÁBRICA DE LA LUZ

La Fábrica de la Luz

the col, you can see the higher col of Puerto de Cómpeta.

The descent from Puerto Blanquillo to Fábrica de la Luz is a long, but gradual one, almost 8km along the dirt track. After about 5km pass **Fuente Borriquero**, the fountain of the donkey, a reminder that pack donkeys used these paths to carry minerals from the mines. A kilometre after the fountain there is a dirt track on the right. **Do not take this turning**, but a few metres further on take a path on the right marked with cairns. This steep path winds its way down to **La Fábrica de la Luz**. ▶

Continuing along the main dirt-track would take you down to the road into La Fábrica de la Luz, but adds nearly 4km to the journey.

The Mountains around Nerja

WALK 10
Lucero

Start/Finish	Puerto Blanquillo (1208m)
Distance	10.5km
Height gain	730m (Although the difference in elevation between the start of the walk and the summit is only 570m, due to ups and downs, you will actually climb a cumulative 730m)
Difficulty	5
Time	4hr 30min
Getting there	Drive to the village of Cómpeta. Do not enter the village but proceed in the direction of Canillas de Albaida. Follow the sign for the recreation area of La Fábrica de la Luz just before the village. After about 2km, just as the road enters the national park, take an unsignposted road to the right. At the first hairpin bend (after just a few hundred metres) take the dirt-track road off this bend to the left. (If you need to ask directions, ask for Puerto Blanquillo (blan-ki-yo).) After half an hour's drive over 10km of rough track, which must be taken slowly to avoid punctures, the road eventually arrives at a bend at a col (///blasts.graphs.imposing), where the rock is white. (5km before this, there is a fountain with good water.)
Options	Can be combined with Walk 9 to make a 7–8hr round trip or Walk 11 to include an ascent of La Chapa.
Warning	This is a walk for a calm day with little wind. It is also not suitable for those who suffer from vertigo.

Of all of the mountain summits of the Axarquía, Lucero is the most impressive. Climbing its precipitous path and arriving at the top of this inverted cone gives a real sense of achievement as well as great views to the Sierra Nevada and down to the coast. It is one of the 'must dos' in Andalucía.

Several routes lead to Lucero, but there is only one path to the summit. What is featured here, in order to encourage anyone doubtful, is the simplest and easiest route. It involves a long drive over a rough dirt-track road to the base of the mountain so that the climb to the summit is then quite short and straightforward.

WALK 10 – LUCERO

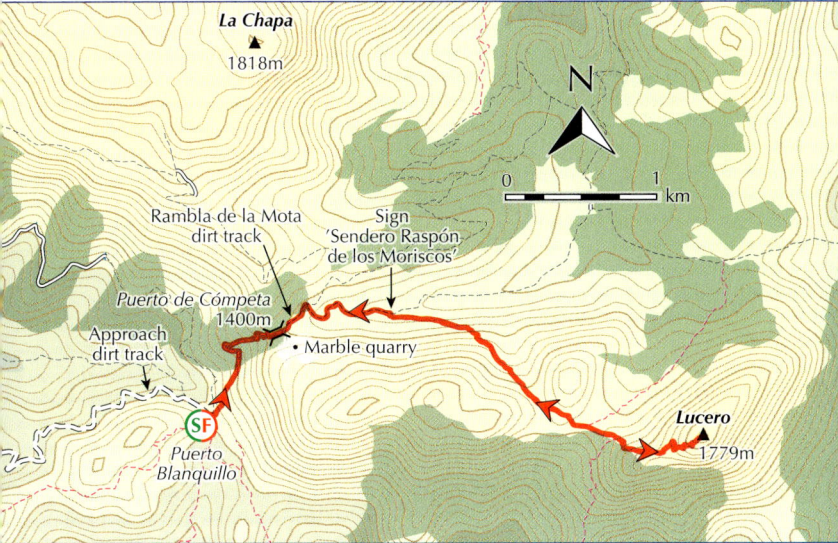

Above the col there is a view over and up to Puerto de Cómpeta. To the left, looking directly north, it should be possible to pick out a waymark, a wooden stake directing you to climb the white rock. This is the path to be followed.

The path makes its way through a pine forest, up to a col, **Puerto de Cómpeta**, at 1400m. There is a sign saying *Fin de Sendero* (end of the walk). Continue on the path, descending to a dirt track which is known as **Rambla de la Mota**. Pass the **Cantera de Mármol** (marble quarry), also known as Cantera del Macho, which stopped producing white marble and blue limestone in 2010.

After 1.5km you will see the **signpost** for the *Sendero Raspón de los Moriscos* (the path to the jagged peak of the converted Moors) to Lucero. The sign informs that it is two hours to the summit from here. There are waymarks all the way to the top.

The gradient is gentle and the route enters a valley to the west of the mountain. It is only when the path passes through this valley that Lucero itself comes into view.

The approach to Lucero

The smaller pointed peak is **Lucerillo**. *Lucero* means bright star, and *lucerillo* means bright little star. The col between the two is known as *Coladero de los Mosquitos*, but there are never likely to be any in this windy patch.

The path to the summit of **Lucero** is not demanding and there is no scrambling, but there is a sheer drop to one side of it.

At the summit there is a surprise – a ruined brick structure. This was a **military post** built, during the Spanish Civil War, by the Franco side. Lookouts had views in all directions, watching for any movements of the Maquis, Republican forces moving through the mountains. The view to the south, towards the sea, may be disappointing because the sun may be shining directly at Lucero. But it is possible to look over to the Sierra Nevada in the east and to La Maroma in the west.

At Puerto de Cómpeta there is the option, instead of going down to Puerto Blanquillo, of turning to the right and climbing to La Chapa (Walk 11).

The only option is to return to **Puerto Blanquillo** via the path of ascent. Once again, care is required on this precipitous descent. ◀

WALK 11
Cerro de la Chapa

Start/Finish	Puerto Blanquillo (1208m)
Distance	11km
Height gain	600m
Difficulty	4
Time	5hr
Getting there	Drive to the village of Cómpeta. Do not enter the village but proceed in the direction of Canillas de Albaida. Follow the sign for the recreation area of La Fábrica de la Luz just before the village. After about 2km, just as the road enters the national park, take an unsignposted road to the right. At the first hairpin bend (after just a few hundred metres) take the dirt-track road off this bend to the left (If you need to ask directions, ask for Puerto Blanquillo (blan-ki-yo).) After half an hour's drive over 10km of rough track, which must be taken slowly, the road eventually arrives at a bend at a col, where the rock is white (///blasts.graphs.imposing).
Options	This walk can be combined with Walk 9.

Looking up from Nerja at the conical summit of Lucero you can see a mountain tucked in behind it that appears to be lower and has a humped summit. This is Cerro de la Chapa. It is actually higher than Lucero but is less exposed and therefore a better choice for a windy day.

This is not a waymarked walk, but it's an easy route through pine forests and open land on an almost continuous track.

At **Puerto Blanquillo** there is a waymark post on the northern side of the col. ▶ Follow the path that is marked by these posts for 600m over rocky ground, but **do not follow them into the forest**.

Immediately short of the pine forest there is a path junction. Take the right-hand option. The path, initially covered in pine needles, winds its way over rocky ground to **Puerto de Cómpeta**.

Puerto Blanquillo (meaning the white gateway/pass) is aptly named, for the rock here is bright white.

THE MOUNTAINS AROUND NERJA

Here there are two options. Either continue down to a dirt track and follow it, turning left at the next junction, or take a shortcut left to ascend the open firebreak. The shortcut up the firebreak – the more straightforward of the options – emerges onto a dirt track where you turn left. Follow this dirt track for 4km.

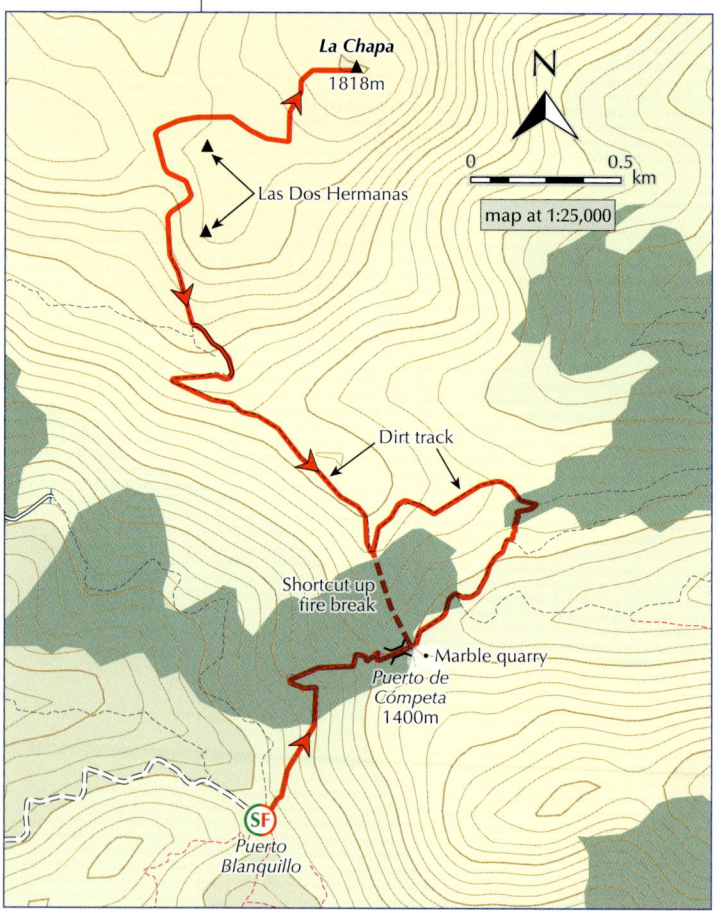

The summit structure on La Chapa

The track winds its way around two peaks known as Las Dos Hermanas (The Two Sisters) and, when rounding the second peak, the goal comes into view. It is well marked by a steel cairn with an aerial. The path eventually breaks up and the final climb to the summit of **La Chapa** is over bare rock.

From the summit (1818m) there is a very good view of Lucero and the path to its summit. **Cerro de la Chapa** is on a ridge that is over 1km long, with Cerro de los Majanos (1806m) at its northern extremity.

Retrace your steps back to find the dirt track and follow it down, eventually joining the **firebreak** down to Puerto de Cómpeta. For a gentler descent, stay on the dirt track when you reach the firebreak, walking east. At the first track junction, turn right and this path will come down to the base of the **Cantera de Mármol** (marble quarry). Climb back up the short distance to **Puerto de Cómpeta** and retrace your steps to **Puerto Blanquillo**.

WALK 12
The oak forest of Salares

Start/Finish	Puente Árabe (Arab bridge), Salares
Distance	7.5km
Height gain	315m
Difficulty	2
Time	3hr
Getting there	Get there either from Vélez-Málaga via Canillas de Aceituno or up from Algarrobo and Sayalonga. Just southeast of Sedella, Salares is in two parts and there is no vehicular access between them. Leave your car on the lower section, where there is a fine car park (///ditches.stakeholder.wildcard). Unfortunately, there are no signs, so it may be necessary to ask '¿Dónde está el sendero para el Puente Árabe?' (Where is the path to the Arab Bridge?)
Options	The latter section of the walk is through housing areas and is not as interesting as the early section, so you could opt to retrace your steps from Casa de Jaro instead.

This sheltered and undulating walk can be enjoyed whatever the weather. It leads from a tiny but delightful village through orange and olive groves and oak woodland to a viewpoint at over 900m. The route is waymarked but the waymarks are not always very regular. Expect to meet nobody for the first hour.

Salares (*sal* in Spanish means salt) gets its name from being the centre for the distribution of salt that was brought up from the coast. It is the smallest village in the Axarquía. With a dwindling population (it boasted 600+ souls in 1990 and was down to 175 in 2022) there is very little employment and many houses are empty.

WALK 12 – THE OAK FOREST OF SALARES

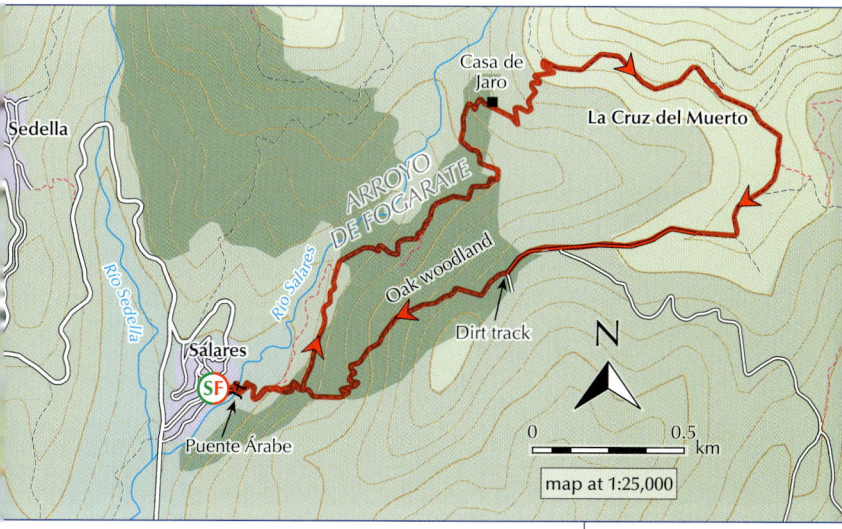

Salares' most important tourist attractions are its minaret and the Moorish bridge. The minaret is also Moorish, in the Mudéjar style, with an intricate lace relief on each face.

In the smallest village of the Axarquía it should not be difficult to find the Arab bridge. ▶ Just over the bridge is the start of the walk. The sign indicates that it is 6.1km and will take three hours. Some would say it's a bit further than that and the timing is a bit optimistic too.

Through groves of orange, almond and olive trees, the walk follows a narrow path that rises and falls as it travels through the Arroyo de Fogarate. Before long you arrive in an **oak woodland**.

This particular species of oak, or **holm oak**, differs from the northern European oaks in that it does not grow to a significant height; the grain on its bark is tighter; the leaves are tiny and the sides of the leaves are not curved; but there is no mistaking the acorns.

Although some guides refer to it as a Roman bridge, it is known locally as the bridge of the Arabs.

THE MOUNTAINS AROUND NERJA

View towards Salares from Casa de Jaro

There are fine views back to the village along the trail. Follow the path down to cross the river and climb steeply up to **Casa de Jaro**, now just a collection of old ruins on a plateau overlooking the valley. The trail circles up over the ruins and rises up to meet a dirt-track road. The hard climb is now over and the remainder of the walk contours around the ridge before descending.

La Cruz del Muerto (the cross of the dead man) is the area at the top of the walk, but the skyline is dominated by a modern villa, apparently unperturbed by the name.

You will need to pay close attention to the waymarks here, keeping right and not descending to the main road. The path returns into the **oak forest** and rejoins the outward path.

WALK 13
Cómpeta to Los Pradillos

Start/Finish	About 1km outside Cómpeta, off the road to Casa de la Mina
Distance	14km
Height gain	410m
Difficulty	3
Time	4hr
Getting there	Drive to Cómpeta via Torrox, but do not enter the village. As you approach the final col before the village you will pass two building materials' depots on the right, one after the other. Then, almost immediately after, at the 4km road marker, turn to the right (beyond the junction on the left there is a pub and a hardware shop). This road, a mixture of concrete and dirt track, goes to Casa de la Mina. Three kilometres along the road you will come to a col where there is a picnic area, a viewpoint (*mirador*) and a small building. This is Puerto del Collado at 890m (///charted.transmitted.subdivision). The mirador is dedicated to Pepe Arjona and his son, José María, who were park rangers. You can park at this picnic spot.
Options	If you have two cars and can leave one at Casa de la Mina the last climb can be avoided. There is a good restaurant here (at the Hotel Casa de la Mina).
Note	It would be a mistake to go to Casa de la Mina and attempt to do this walk in reverse. The markers are not designed for this option.

This route is a walk back in time into wild valleys that once supported a community of mining people. The settlement was also used during the Civil War when the Maquis hid here from Franco's forces.

This is an undulating walk over rough ground. Although the difficulty rating is low, stiff boots with ankle supports are recommended. There is a waymarked walk entitled Casa de la Mina - Los Pradillos, which has been used as the basis for this walk. However, the waymarked walk has been modified because the starting point is difficult to find and there are precious few places to park there.

There are numerous paths and dirt tracks in these mountains and it is important to watch out for the markers and follow them. You will be switching from wide dirt tracks to narrow paths and back again.

◀ From the mirador there is a road to the right that descends to Casa de la Mina – this is your return road. To start the walk take the road to the left. However, if you want to shorten the journey you have the option of climbing the steep scree just to the right of it, between the two roads leading north. You can do this a second time to cut out the next zig-zag.

Eventually you will meet a dirt track coming from the left, with waymarkers on it. Follow this road. The coloured waymarkers are for a part of the GR 249, from Cómpeta to Frigiliana. Follow the plain waymarkers; they will shortly take you to a col where there is a high-tension electricity pylon.

> You will have the option of returning to this col on the return journey. It is known as **El Collado de Huerta Grande**, the col of the big market garden. Some 200m below the col are buildings. The large one with the rooflight is Hotel Casa de la Mina and to the right of it is Casa de la Mina. There is a narrow path that goes from the col down to these buildings. This is the optional return route.

Proceed along the dirt track following the waymarkers, then leave it and follow along a narrow path. You should be keep an eye out for the *cabra montés*. The trail is through pine trees with the predominant low shrubs being rosemary.

After a while you will reach another col where there is a path to the left that goes to Fábrica de la Luz. This is **Cruz de Canillas**. Fifty metres beyond this junction there is a ruin on the side of the trail. This is **Cortijo María Dolores** (the farmhouse of Mary of the Sorrows).

After another few kilometres you reach your goal – the old settlement of **Los Pradillos**.

> The first structure to be encountered in **Los Pradillos** is a lime kiln. The insides of the limestone walls would have been plastered in clay. Further up on the right are old mine shafts, now blocked.

WALK 13 – CÓMPETA TO LOS PRADILLOS

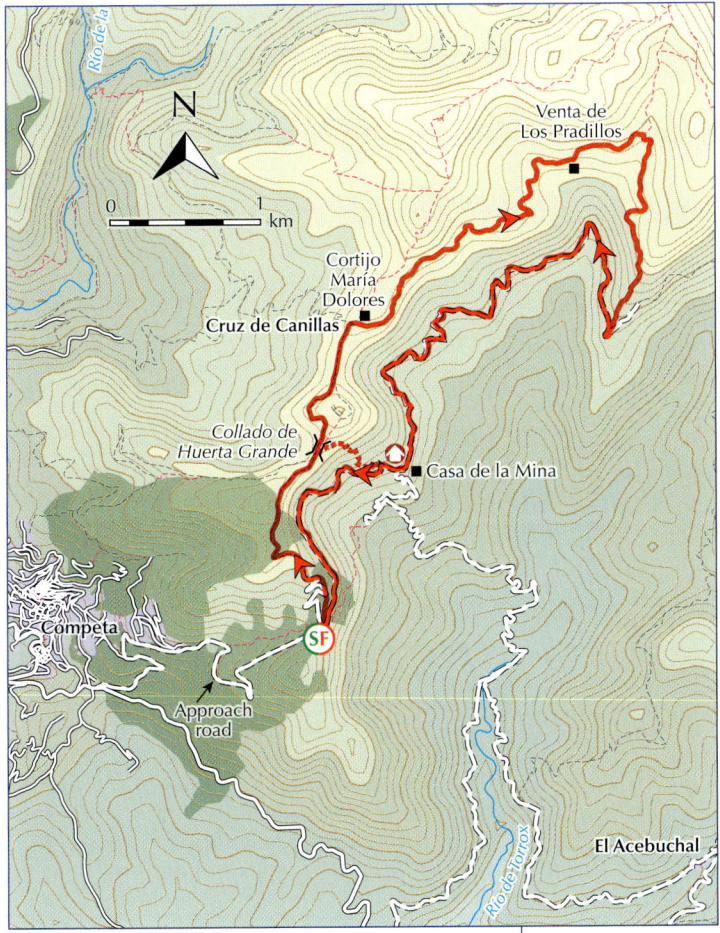

Next the path comes to the main enclosure of Los Pradillos. It is on an elevated spot, with views down into the valley.

View of the era at Los Pradillos

On the map it is marked as **Venta de Los Pradillos**, meaning the Inn of Little Pasture Lands. There were many inns along paths such as this to afford shelter to travellers.

On the north side of the walled enclosure there is an impressive circular flat area (*era*) that would have had multiple uses: threshing, laying out *esparto* (coarse high grass) for weaving, as well as an ideal social and play area. Above the settlement is an extensive area of esparto used for making baskets, hats and ropes (*maroma*). Above the esparto fields there is yet another lime kiln, and further up there is yet another ruined building.

These mountains were popular hiding areas for the Maquis during the Civil War. Importantly, Los Pradillos is not visible from the summit of Lucero. On that mountain there was a lookout constructed specifically to monitor the movement of the Maquis in the mountains (see Walk 10).

WALK 13 – CÓMPETA TO LOS PRADILLOS

The walk descends to cross a riverbed. Do not follow the riverbed but climb out on the other side. The route has now left the coloured waymarkers of the GR 249, and is following the plain waymarkers. You will need to push through 2km of narrow track with the rosemary and gorse scraping your legs. The track eventually emerges onto a wide dirt track, which you follow around a hairpin bend. ▸ This wide dirt track goes all the way back to Hotel Casa de la Mina. When the hotel is open it is an excellent stop for coffee or a snack/meal.

Looking back there is a fine vista of Lucero and you can just imagine Franco's men up there during the Civil War peering through their binoculars.

THE VENTAS OF ANDALUCÍA

A *venta* is an inn or hostelry. Throughout the country many of these ventas were positioned at strategic junctions of paths and these afforded shelter to the traveller. Of course, they also served as eating and drinking houses for the locals.

During the Civil War the ventas in the countryside were seen by Franco as places frequented by the Maquis, and so he ordered for them to be destroyed. In 1940 many thousands of ventas, such as this one at Los Pradillos, were burnt to the ground.

Just across the road from the venta the **Casa de la Mina** was the industrial centre of mining in the area.

From here, proceed along the dirt track to arrive back at your car. Alternatively, those with energy to spare could take a right and follow along a steep track up to Collado de Huerta Grande and return to their car from there.

WALK 14
Malascamas from La Fábrica de la Luz

Start/Finish	La Fábrica de la Luz
Distance	22km
Height gain	1135m
Difficulty	8
Time	7hr 30min
Getting there	Take the motorway and exit to Cómpeta, winding up the many hairpin bends to the village. Do not enter the village but bypass it in the direction of Canillas de Albaida. This is a mere 2km further on. As you approach Canillas watch out for the signs to the recreation area of La Fábrica de la Luz – it is before you enter the village. At La Fábrica de la Luz (the factory of light, but the term used for electricity generation) there should be ample parking (///overhaul.affronts.edicts).
Options	There are many options to shorten the walk.

This is a long walk in the most remote area of the sierra. Get acquainted with the maze of tracks in the region. At 22km and a height gain of 1135m this is one of the most arduous of the walks in this book. Malascamas (1793m) is the fourth highest of the mountains to be climbed, after La Maroma (2069m), Navachica (1831m) and La Chapa (1818m).

The name Malascamas means poor, or bad, beds. Like Navachica the mountain is situated deep inside the sierra, and to get to it involves quite a long walk. Of course, if you have the luxury of an SUV you can actually drive all the way to the col under the summit. Even with a saloon car the walk can be shortened, as long as you are brave enough to drive on the rough tracks.

Park at **La Fábrica de la Luz** and walk to and over the river. Climb the steep concrete road. After half an hour you will reach a dirt track coming from the right. This will be your return route. (You can actually drive to this point,

WALK 14 – MALASCAMAS FROM LA FÁBRICA DE LA LUZ

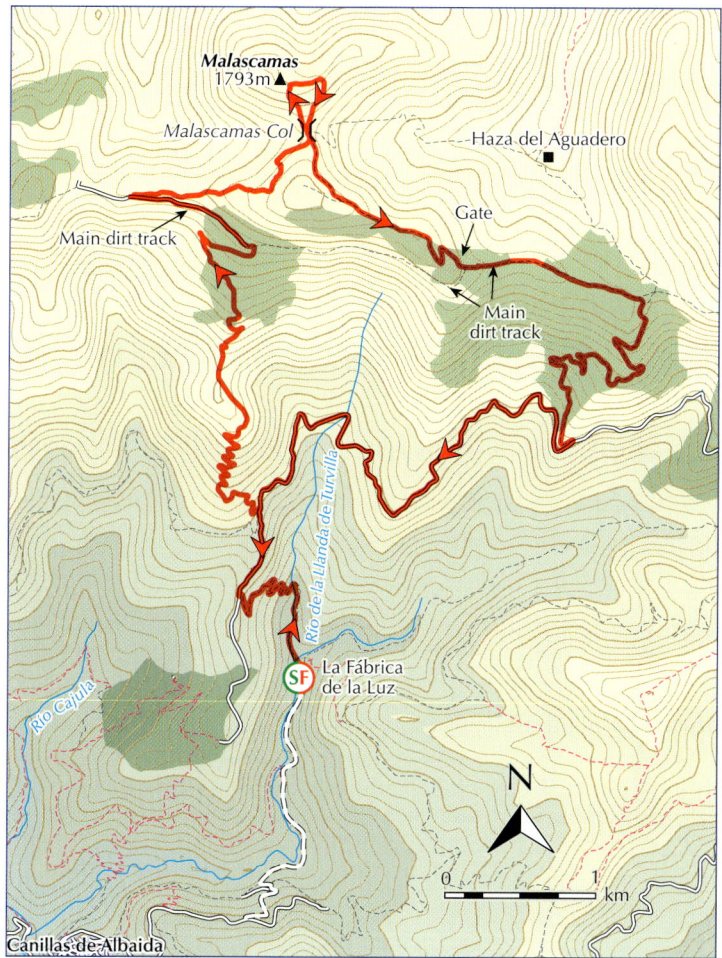

park your car and start the walk here). Turn left and climb to eventually reach a flat section. Off to the right you will see a large house. Turn right towards the right-hand side of the entrance gate to the house. Zig-zag north until you

THE MOUNTAINS AROUND NERJA

Cork bark stripped

Some of the oak trees on this route have had their bark harvested to make cork for bottles and other purposes.

From here to the col under the summit you will need your navigation skills.

Be aware of inhospitable vegetation.

meet the main track that traverses along, or close to, the ridge of the mountain, shown as a road on the map. The aim is to get over the high land north of this road, and then descend to the col under Malascamas summit. ◄

Part of the climb follows a dirt track that zig-zags through a firebreak. One option would be to climb the firebreak; it's a steeper climb, but it shortens the journey.

Turn left at the main dirt track. ◄ Just before entering the trees you turn sharp right, coming off the main dirt track, and climb towards a col on the right that has standing rocks. The paths here are ill-defined. Go through the pass in the rocks at the col and, beyond it, follow a rough path climbing to the east. You can either climb this path to its top and descend to the Malascamas col, or find a way down to the col without climbing to the top. ◄

WALK 14 – MALASCAMAS FROM LA FÁBRICA DE LA LUZ

Malascamas. The peak on the left is the highest point on the west–east ridge

Once you reach the **Malascamas col** you can approach directly to the **Malascamas summit**, climbing over scree and loose rock. Alternatively, take the path to the right (east) that circles to the summit. ▶

From the summit it is best to follow the path to the east, rather than descending the steep scree.

One option for this walk is to return the same way you ascended, but the route shown on the map takes you off to the east. Standing at the col, with Malascamas behind you, there are several tracks: the first one on the left descends east towards Haza del Aguadero (Walk 28); but the route to take – the second one on the left – swings off to the southeast on a gradual slope.

Much of the return route is up and down through wooded areas. ▶ Follow the dirt track and pass through a gate to rejoin the main track and continue to head east. Descending this main dirt track, go right at the junctions you meet, heading first south, then west. Eventually, after crossing the **Río de la Llanda de Turvilla**, you will arrive back at the junction passed on the way up. Once again, there is the option of descending the steep firebreak to shorten the return journey to **La Fábrica de la Luz**.

At the summit, as you look over to La Maroma, you might reflect on where the mountain got the name: bad beds.

Look out for the wild boar that roam here, although it would be unusual to see any.

LA MAROMA

La Maroma from Lake Viñuela

Summit routes at a glance

Walk number/ start	Elevation at start	Height gain	Distance	Walk time	Drive from Nerja*
15 Salares	1600m	560m	12km	4hr 30min	1hr 30min
16 Canillas de Aceituno	649m	1420m	18km	7hr	1hr
17 Alcaucín	846m	1225m	16km	6hr 30min	45min
18 Sedella	824m	1245m	17km	7hr	1hr
19 Alcaicería	1107m	960m	15km	6hr	1hr 30min

* each way

LA MAROMA

La Maroma is the highest of the mountains in the province of Málaga, at 2069m. At the top its spine is flat – the section that is above 2000m is over 1km long and the section that is higher than 1900m is nearly 4km. There are four paths to the summit: from the southeast via Sedella, from the southwest via Canillas de Aceituno, from the west via Alcaucín and El Alcázar, and finally from the northeast via Alcaicería and Cortijo Robledal. (There is a fifth route from the east, but this requires a four-wheel drive vehicle from Salares – see Walk 15.) The routes are quite dissimilar, each with its own challenges and characteristics. A sixth option is possible from Alcaucín village, via Torrecilla de La Maroma (see Walk 22), but this would be a climb of 1500m and a walk time of 9hr 30min.

The name La Maroma refers to a rope made of reed/rush, or in Spanish *esparto*. The esparto grows all over the region. It will be seen interspersed with the gorse, broom and rosemary or on its own in thick clumps. It is used for thatching and weaving baskets and hats. The long summit is Loma de Las Víboras, the spine of the vipers.

ROUTES TO THE SUMMIT

The least onerous way to summit La Maroma is via Salares. However, an SUV is required to negotiate the steep, dirt track access road. Of the other four routes the option via Alcaicería is the longest drive, but the shortest walk and climb. This climb, in winter months, may require crampons, because it is on the north

Characteristics

Need an SUV to access start. Easy parking. 150m of downhill. Water sources near start and finish.

Second most popular route. Parking might not be as easy as others. Longest walk, highest climb. Path easy to follow. Water at Rabita.

Slightly shorter drive than the others. Easy parking and toilets. Waymarked walk is much longer, and alternative shorter route is tricky. Water at start only.

Least popular route. Steep, precipitous access road. Easy parking and toilets. Steep climb in final gully. Water at start only.

Most popular route with relatively gentle gradient all the way. Impressive views through the Zafarraya pass, and easy parking. Spectacular climb through Salto de Caballo. No water sources.

THE MOUNTAINS AROUND NERJA

La Maroma covered with a blanket of snow

side of the mountain. But, of the four, it is the most spectacular climb.

When you arrive at the summit, do not forget to look at the Casa de la Nieve (literally house of snow), a deep crevice/hole in the rock, where, during winter, snow was gathered and compacted to form ice. The surface was then insulated with straw and left. During the hot summer days workers would trek up the mountain with donkeys to bring down the ice.

At the base of La Maroma there is a fine cable bridge that is worthwhile going to. Two different routes to this bridge (Walks 20 and 21) are included. Last in this section is a fine walk to the southwest shoulder of La Maroma, which is Torrecilla de La Maroma (Walk 22).

A WORD OF CAUTION

Whichever route is taken up La Maroma, vigilance at the summit is required to remember the direction of approach. When mist envelopes the summit it is very easy to become disorientated. Over the bare summit rock there are no paths and waymarks are scarce.

WALK 15
La Maroma from Salares

Start/Finish	near Salares
Distance	12km
Height gain	560m
Difficulty	5
Time	4hr 30min
Getting there	The general directions are: Algarrobo, then Sayalonga, Árchez and Salares. Come off the motorway in the direction of Algarrobo; pass through the village and through the next village which is Sayalonga; after about 4km go left in the direction of Árchez, but do not enter this village; instead go left, then right to arrive at the village of Salares. Do not enter the village, but bypass the lower entrance to Salares and rise to take the first right. You will arrive at a ceramic walled welcome sign to Salares: *Bienvenidos*. Take the first left after this (///globe.exploratory.marvel). Because of the approach route's complexity, **a map and GPX file can be downloaded from** www.cicerone.co.uk/1176 (see 'Updates' tab for the map – print it at as large a scale as possible; see 'Downloads' tab for the GPX route – save it to your smartphone/device). Generally, you need to climb, follow the obvious road, and take left-hand options at junctions. The drive is an adventure in itself. You will eventually pass through an open gate and arrive on flat ground. When you pass through the remnants of another gateway, take the dirt track to the left, driving over flat ground to park on grass (///gravest.consulates.inbound). The elevation here is 1597m.
Options	Visit the well at Tacita de Plata. View the deep cave on the summit.

Although this is the shortest walk up to the summit of La Maroma there are a number of drawbacks. First of all, you will need an SUV or off-road vehicle to negotiate the long, steep and rough approach track. Secondly, this track is difficult to navigate (download the map and GPX file for the

THE MOUNTAINS AROUND NERJA

approach before you leave). And, finally, there is a 150m descent to add to the difference in elevation. Nevertheless, this is a very pleasant walk.

This used to be a waymarked track, but, at time of publication there were only a handful of waymarkers left, and there were none near the start.

◄ Follow the dirt track, then descend to the right on a narrow path. Just after the bottom of the descent there is a **trough** with running water. In February the trough will have many tadpoles in it. Next, the path zig-zags up to a col on a ridge. Turn to the left at the **col** and the summit of La Maroma will come into view. Unfortunately, you need to descend some more before you tackle the long climb to the summit. The route passes close to the path for **Tacita de Plata**, a well with water flowing into a trough. After that you will join the route that comes up from Robledal (Walk 19).

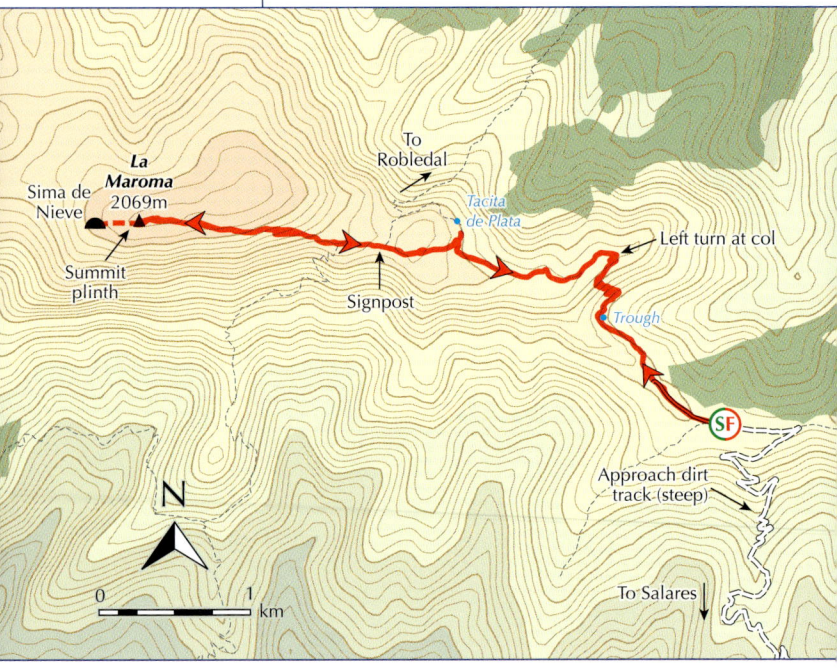

WALK 15 – LA MAROMA FROM SALARES

Descending from La Maroma, with the snow outlining the horizontal path to follow just under the ridge

The route passes over bare rock, precipitous in places, before reaching the final climb.

If you bypass the **La Maroma summit plinth** and descend to the west, you will see a fenced enclosure with a deep **cave**. It used to be the custom to fill the cave with snow in winter. The snow was compacted and eventually formed into ice. The surface was then covered with a thick layer of straw. During the hot summer the straw was regularly stripped back and blocks of ice were taken down the mountain.

There is no other option but to return the way you ascended. Remember that you are heading east towards Tacita de Plata, then continuing east to the ridge you ascended at the beginning of the walk.

WALK 16
La Maroma from Canillas de Aceituno

Start/Finish	Canillas de Aceituno
Distance	18km
Height gain	1420m
Difficulty	6
Time	7hr
Getting there	Drive to the village of Canillas de Aceituno. At the first roundabout instead of taking the main road into the village take the road to the left of it. Just after you cross the bridge there is a municipal car park on the left where the walk will start (///remembers.commentators.comparisons).

This walk starts from the historic and attractive village of Canillas de Aceituno and visits the old Moorish settlement of La Rabita before climbing to the prominent domed summit of La Maroma. The ascent is long but straightforward, waymarked all the way and with plenty of interest en route.

CANILLAS DE ACEITUNO

The direct translation of Canillas de Aceituno is taps of the olive, but this is not the origin of the name. From ancient Arabic, *canillas* was a place where cane grew, and *aceituno* has been distorted from the Arabic for silk. The village has a fine Roman bridge and an interesting cave, Cueva Fagara, where Neolithic remains were found. There is a restaurant (La Maroma) near the start of the walk, but to sense the history of the village, visit La Sociedad, the first place in Spain to establish a workers' cooperative; it is now a restaurant popular with the locals.

From the car park, walk up a steep **stone ramp** that leads to a series of steps. At the top turn right and follow further steps, all the time heading in the same northeasterly direction. There are multiple choices, but rest assured that they all eventually lead to the start of the walk. ◄

There are steps en route that have a wooden handrail on the side.

WALK 16 – LA MAROMA FROM CANILLAS DE ACEITUNO

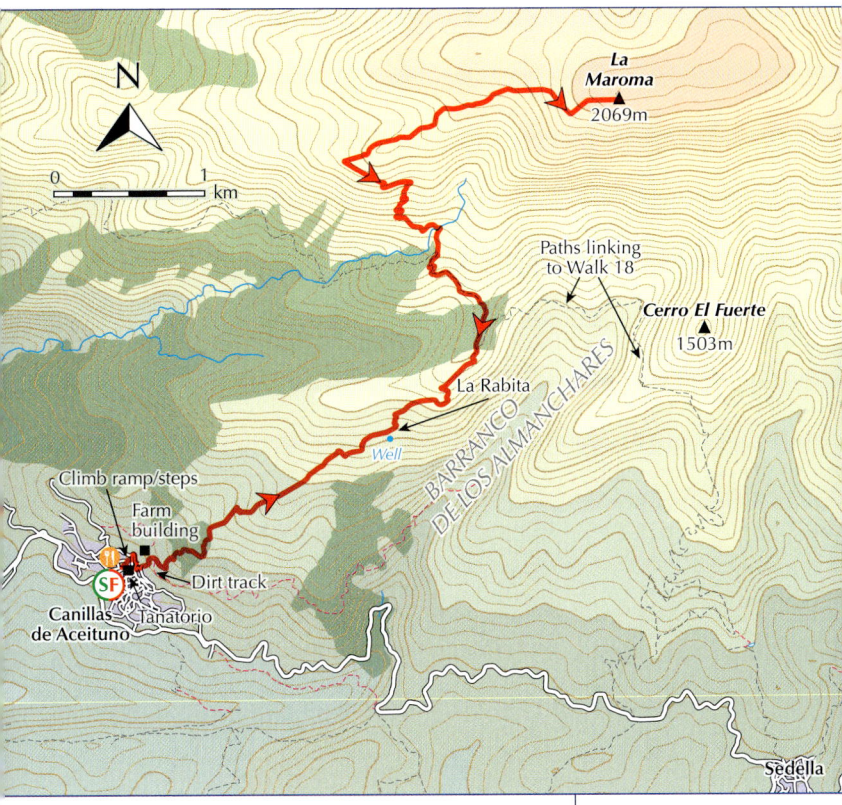

Follow the sign for a *sendero* (path) to Casa de la Nieve (the house of snow). This is the local name for the summit of La Maroma – it originated from the custom of storing snow and ice in a cave on the summit. The first sign suggests that the walk is only 6km, but the sign further up is more correct at 9km. Remember that this is the distance to the summit of La Maroma and does not include the return.

This is a waymarked path all the way to the summit. ▶

The moderate gradient winds through pines and *esparto* over micaceous (green) shale in between outcrops of limestone.

THE MOUNTAINS AROUND NERJA

Towards La Maroma, leaving the shelter of the pines

There is a well here that has good water in it.

After 45 minutes the path reaches the old settlement of **La Rabita**. ◄ Further along the trail there is a cave, and from the cave the ruins of old buildings can be seen.

A sign near the cave tells walkers that **La Rabita** was frequented by the Romans from 100BC to AD300. Later, in AD700, it was settled by the Moors and there was a working mine here. The area later features in the annals of the Morisco (converted Muslim) rebellion and punishment (1560). The water from the well was once piped to Canillas de Aceituno and you will have wandered over some of the old ceramic pipes en route. In the springtime the stone trough below the well will be teeming with tadpoles.

WALK 16 – LA MAROMA FROM CANILLAS DE ACEITUNO

Summit of La Maroma

From an elevation of approximately 1200m, the enormous hump of La Maroma fills the vista. However, there is no need to be alarmed – the route does not head straight up its vertical face, but circles to the north to approach the summit from the west. ▶ The path that crosses the **Barranco de los Almanchares** can clearly be seen on the right as it descends to the road between Canillas de Aceituno and Sedella.

At an elevation of about 1300m, the path passes to the right of the ruins of an old stone beehive *refugio* (refuge), and further up there is a smaller refugio below the trail on the right. There is a well at Los Charcones, but the flow out of it is very poor and therefore suspect.

The trail zig-zags out to the west and, when it eventually makes the turn to the east, is at an elevation of 1700m with only a little over 300m and a relatively flat 2km to go to the summit of **La Maroma**.

Coming down from the summit on this path poses few dangers and there are no particularly steep sections. The route is obvious almost all the way. However, upon arrival at the outskirts of **Canillas de Aceituno** there is no clear path to the car park. If you can't remember exactly how to get back to the car park, don't worry too much – walking through private property is something the locals are used to and they are very friendly about it.

> Droppings on the path indicate that the *cabra montés* grazes here.

The Mountains around Nerja

WALK 17
La Maroma from Alcaucín

Start/Finish	El Alcázar recreation area
Distance	16km
Height gain	1225m
Difficulty	7
Time	6hr 30min
Getting there	Alcaucín is off the road from Vélez-Málaga going north. Pass the signposts for Viñuela and later take the road to the right to Alcaucín. Just as it enters the village there is a road to the left signposted for the recreation area of El Alcázar, 5km along a dirt-track road. At El Alcázar, park at the highest of the car parks (///whichever.announcement.essay) and you'll find a sign describing the walk.
Options	Follow the waymarked longer version of the route for a gentler gradient but a round-trip distance of 21km.

The El Alcázar recreation area is popular for school outings and for picnics. The route described here shortcuts the waymarked path that is used by loggers and is known as Castillones. The shortcut saves 6km in total but it is steeper and not as well defined. It also takes in a good variety of surfaces, vegetations and vistas.

Walk up the stone steps from the car park and go through the picnic area, up alongside a fast-flowing water channel, to a wide track with waymarks. Follow the waymarked route until it reaches a chain over the road and swings left (this is the longer route). At the first junction, beside a waymark, take the path that goes off to the right (this is the shorter route, described below).

The path turns into a narrow track, winding its way through the trees and along the face of the rock. When you arrive at a grove of tall pines (critical point), walk up

WALK 17 – LA MAROMA FROM ALCAUCÍN

through them – although the pine needles will obscure the path.

The **spine**, which takes over half an hour to climb, is a firebreak. The route follows little cairns, until it rejoins the waymarked **Castillones track** at a col where there is a galvanised **rain funnel**. You are now on the **Loma de las Víboras**, the hill of the vipers. Below and to the east you can see the waymarked road. Turn right, following the waymarkers towards the summit of La Maroma, but first you will have to cross two false summits. ▶

As you approach the final summit plateau of **La Maroma** the path is ill-defined and there are no more waymarkers, but there is very little vegetation. Over the summit, which is reminiscent of the Burren in County Clare in Ireland, you cross a karst limestone pavement, with holes and caverns in it formed by mildly acidic waters reacting with and dissolving the limestone.

The limestone in places is friable and weathered and there are places where you can rest in the shade and out of the wind.

The Mountains around Nerja

Walkers on the summit plateau of La Maroma

The return to **El Alcázar** is not as complicated as the ascent as it is easier to notice the vagaries of the path. You also have the option of taking the longer, more leisurely route down the **Castillones track**, thus avoiding the steep spine descent.

A WORD OF CAUTION: LEAVING ALCAUCÍN

Before leaving Alcaucín by car, note that at the first road junction you have a choice between Viñuela/Vélez-Málaga to the left or Granada to the right. The left option follows a narrow, twisting road for many kilometres. For the most direct route to the coast go right towards Granada, crossing a long bridge. The road comes to the main road where there is a left turn back to Vélez-Málaga and the motorway.

WALK 18
La Maroma from Sedella

Start/Finish	Sedella recreation area
Distance	17km
Height gain	1245m
Difficulty	7
Time	7hr
Getting there	It takes about the same time to get to Sedella whether you travel via Algarrobo/Sayalonga or via Vélez-Málaga/Canillas de Aceituno. The latter route is longer but involves fewer twisting roads. The concrete road to Sedella recreation area is not easy to find: on the MA-126, at the road junction 7km from Canillas de Aceituno and 2km short of Sedella, signposts point south to Los Valverdes and Rubite. Take the steep, concrete road going north until you reach the recreation area (///mortgage.evidently.provided), where there is ample parking and toilets.
Note	Avoid this walk if you are nervous about driving on a narrow, precipitous road.

This walk starts at the Área Recreativa de Sedella at an elevation of 824m. A suitable road has only recently been built to connect it with the village of Sedella, a distance of over 2km and a climb of 165m; the journey still takes over an hour. Before this road was installed a 4WD vehicle was needed, or else the walk from Sedella to La Maroma was quite a marathon.

From the **recreation area** there are two paths, one to Canillas de Aceituno, via the cable bridge of El Saltillo, and the other to La Maroma. The direction for both is initially the same: head north uphill along a wide dirt track and then follow a sign to La Choza del Guarda. ▶

A little further on you will reach a small, thatched *refugio*. This is **La Choza**, a former lookout hut. The trail up is around to the right from La Choza and follows

> The other sign, Mirador de la Buitrera, refers to a former vulture sanctuary; this route, to the left, goes to Canillas de Aceituno.

Thatched refuge of La Choza en route from Sedella

established, graded dirt tracks, which are rather long and tedious. ◄ Above the open pavement area known as *era* the trail narrows to a path and becomes steeper. Ahead there is an escarpment protruding from the mountain called **El Fuerte** (1509m). The path passes under it at an elevation of 1300m, so you are almost halfway up. ◄

The path arrives on the spine of La Maroma via a **steep gully** and it is important to memorise the features of this junction for the descent. Turn left for the summit of **La Maroma**. ◄

> The **summit plateau** of La Maroma is over 4km long. Its karst surface has many crevices, some quite enormous. The largest of these sinkholes, Sima de Nieve, is all of 45m in depth, and is so called because it fills with snow in the winter and was used, for several months into the spring and summer, as a source of ice. To reach it, carry on walking west, passing the summit plinth, until you see a fenced enclosure.

You may decide to take shortcuts through the switchbacks on the return journey.

En route there is a doubtful water source at 1350m.

If you need water, turn right for Tacita de Plata, where there is a pipe emerging from the rock with a constant flow of good water into a stone trough.

WALK 18 – LA MAROMA FROM SEDELLA

If your transport is at **Sedella recreation area**, there is no other option but to retrace your steps. Care is required on those steep sections, but you can cut through the tedious switchbacks.

If you have made good progress and time is available, it is worth visiting the fine **Roman bridge** on the northeast side of the village. Unfortunately, this entails returning to Sedella and then climbing again.

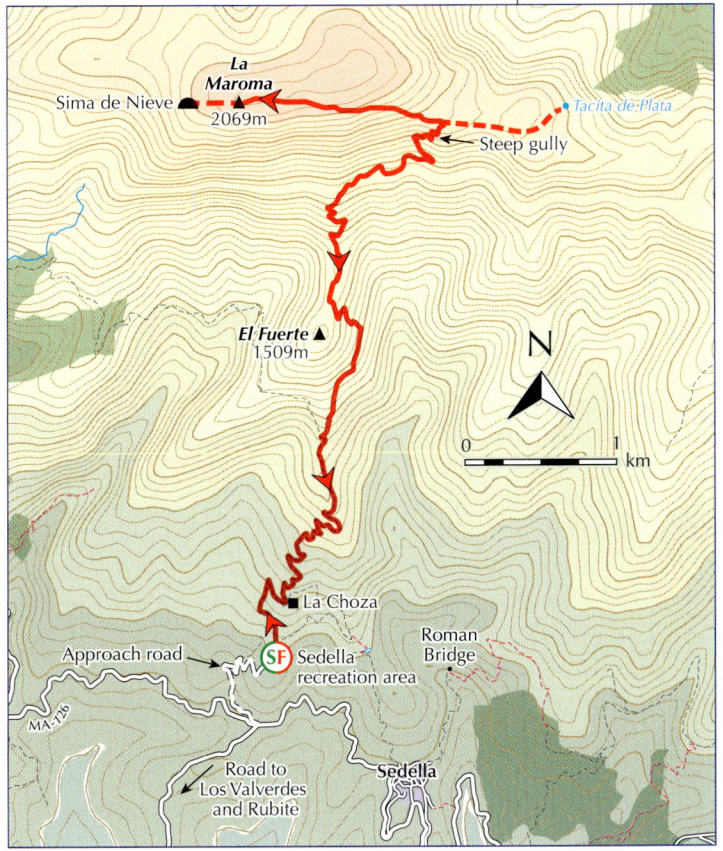

WALK 19
La Maroma from Alcaicería

Start/Finish	Robledal
Distance	15km
Height gain	960m
Difficulty	6
Time	6hr
Getting there	Come off the motorway at Vélez-Málaga and head north in the direction of Alhama de Granada and Zafarraya. The road steepens and passes through a natural pass in the Sierra Tejeda – Ventas de Zafarraya. Some 10km after Zafarraya, the road arrives at Alcaicería. There is a hotel on the road facing the approach. Take the dirt track to the right of the hotel in the direction of Cortijo de Robledal. Ignoring all junctions on the road, after 6km the road reaches the ruin of Robledal and a sign indicates the route. There are plenty of places to park in the shade (///jaundice.wrenches.grasshopper).
Note	Because this approach is from the north, ice and snow may linger on the path in spring and in very cold conditions crampons or microspikes may be required.

This is a waymarked trail, with a consistently gentle gradient all the way to the summit of La Maroma. The long drive in via Ventas de Zafarraya is compensated with spectacular views and a good place to eat at Alcaicería on the way back (Hotel Restaurante Los Caños de la Alcaicería).

Follow the waymarks from the sign at the car park. The route is initially through a pine forest on a gentle gradient passing through **Barranco del Selladero**. It climbs steadily to a bend in the path with a sign pointing to **El Salto de Caballo** (the horse jump), a pass into the flattish area of the mountain.

From here the trail rises to a junction at 1900m, where it passes a gully coming from the left. This is the path from Sedella. Carry on walking over the relatively

WALK 19 – LA MAROMA FROM ALCAICERÍA

flat 2km of stone pavement to the summit of **La Maroma** and the triangulation point.

The top of **La Maroma** contains many deep crevices and the path over the summit pavement is not defined, so care is required in cloudy conditions. The mountain can suddenly be engulfed in cloud with no return path in sight. When the summit is covered in snow there is the added danger of stepping into a hole.

Retrace your outward route back to **Robledal**.

Alternative descent
The well at **Tacita de Plata** is a worthwhile diversion on the descent. Proceed along the path over to the east to reach the well. Below it there is a sign for the alternative path to El Robledal.

The well at Tacita de Plata

A PAUSE FOR REFRESHMENT

The Alcaicería Hotel is a popular, inexpensive eating place and is highly recommended. Outside of the summer months there will be a large fire blazing in the huge fireplace. Look at the stuffed heads of wild boar and wild goat, and maybe buy some local honey, cheese, salami or wine. Near the hotel there is a tiny church up above the road. Below the hotel, on the far side of the road, there is a bullring.

WALK 20
Canillas de Aceituno to the cable bridge

Start/Finish	Canillas de Aceituno
Distance	10km
Height gain	210m
Difficulty	3
Time	3hr 30min
Getting there	Drive towards Málaga and take the exit to Vélez-Málaga. Bypass Vélez and proceed 6km along this road to take the road to the right signposted Canillas de Aceituno. The village is divided into two sections, upper and lower. This walk sets off from the upper section, so take the road to the left as you enter the village. There are places to park your car alongside the *tanatorio* (funeral home), or down the hill before it (///directing.resembling.stimuli).
Options	Continue the walk to Sedella and get a taxi back.

This is an easy walk to a spectacular bridge that can be done in a morning. It is under an hour's drive from Nerja to Canillas de Aceituno and the start of the walk. Then it takes only another 45 minutes of easy walking to get to the bridge. After that there are several options. The walk featured here takes us over the bridge, then to return and detour to a waterfall.

Puente Colgante El Saltillo, to give it its full name (the hanging bridge of the little jump), is a 54m-long cable bridge that hangs 70m above the Río Almanchares. It was built in 2020 and is part of the GR 249 that links Canillas de Aceituno to the village of Sedella.

In **Canillas de Aceituno**, walk past the tanatorio and climb the steps up to the top of the village. ▶ Initially there are no signs for the walk, but eventually you will come to a sign for Sendero La Maroma straight on up, and El Saltillo off to the right. Follow the sign to El Saltillo.

This route is the same as to the start of Walk 16.

The Mountains around Nerja

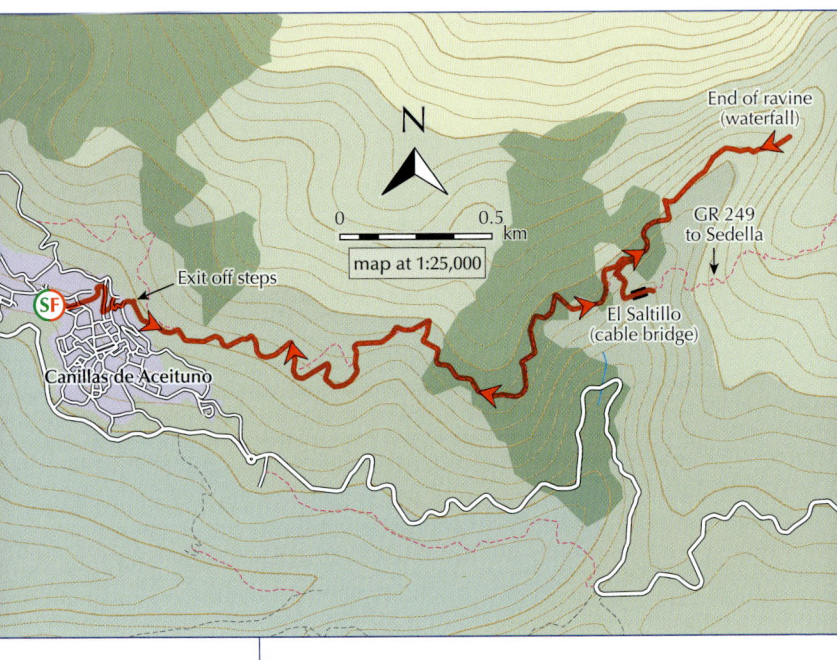

The route is a flat, narrow track through an olive grove. Emerging from the olive grove, follow the path alongside a water channel and head into a ravine. After half an hour you will come through a pass in the limestone and the bridge will be below on your right.

There are 160 steps to negotiate down to the bridge, and, obviously, the same to return.

From the western side of the bridge, continue up the ravine. The path is flat and, after 20 minutes, you will arrive at the end of the ravine. There is a waterfall here and an ideal place for a picnic. ◄

> From the top of the ravine it is a mere 5km and another 150m of climbing to continue over the sierra to Sedella.

If you are hungry on your return, there are some fine restaurants in **Canillas de Aceituno**. The speciality of the area is **roast kid** (goat), or *chivo* in Spanish. Be aware that, when you order chivo, you will be served it in three courses: first the innards, then the head (sliced in half),

WALK 20 – CANILLAS DE ACEITUNO TO THE CABLE BRIDGE

El Saltillo bridge

and finally the remainder. And the Spanish eat all of it, brain, eyes and guts included. On Sundays the village is full of people coming to eat chivo.

WALK 21
Sedella to the cable bridge

Start/Finish	Sedella recreation area
Distance	8km
Height gain	475m
Difficulty	5
Time	3hr 30min
Getting there	The access road to the start is not easy to find. It is on the MA-126 between the villages of Canillas de Aceituno and Sedella, 2km short of Sedella. Coming from Canillas de Aceituno, after approximately 7km, you will reach a crossroads where there is a road descending to the right that is signposted Los Valverdes and Rubite. Directly opposite is a steep concrete road rising to your left. This is the route to take (it is not signposted). Ascend the very steep, narrow concrete road, with deadly drops on one side, until you arrive at a large recreation area, where there is ample parking (///mortgage.evidently.provided).
Options	The visitor centre in Sedella is highly recommended and could also be combined with Walk 12 to the Salares oak forest.

This alternative route to the cable bridge of Saltillo is more interesting and challenging than Walk 20. It takes you up and through the sierra under La Maroma and then descends into the ravine with the cable bridge. The descent into the ravine is steep and precipitous and not suitable for anyone suffering from vertigo. The descent and subsequent ascent is reflected in the medium difficulty rating of 5.

If you have aspirations of climbing La Maroma from Sedella (Walk 18), this walk could act as a precursor, since it commences at the same point.

The visitor centre in Sedella is very well worth a visit. Its displays of scenery, wildlife and walking routes are all particular to the park where all the walks in this book are located. Here you can purchase maps, guidebooks (in Spanish), walking sticks and information sheets. The centre is only open on the mornings of Friday, Saturday and Sunday from 9.30am to 2.30pm.

WALK 21 – SEDELLA TO THE CABLE BRIDGE

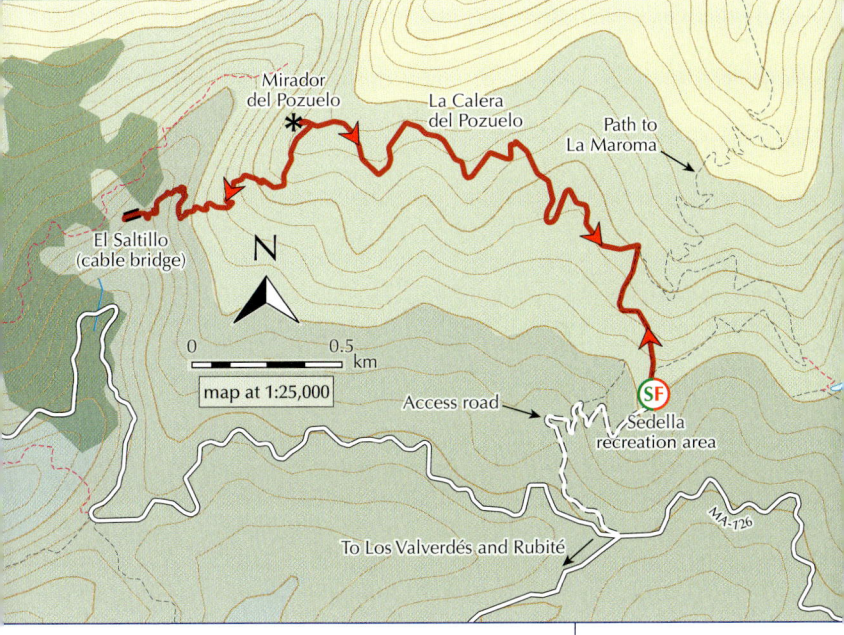

There are picnic tables and toilets at the recreation area. The statue of the wild mountain goat is at the recreation area, and it is the symbol of the **Parque Natural de Sierras Tejeda, Almijara y Alhama**.

Walk 21 is part of the GR 249, Gran Senda de Málaga, and the waymarkers will take you to Canillas de Aceituno, 7.1km to the west. The same starting point and direction also leads to La Maroma.

From the recreation area, walk 1km uphill along a wide dirt track until you arrive at a cross-roads. Signposted to the right is La Choza, a hut on the route up La Maroma (Walk 18). Instead, turn left, following the signpost for the vulture sanctuary. Unfortunately, it is no longer there as it was moved further into the mountains is 2022. ▶

The route passes the hide where ailing griffon vultures used to be fed.

The Mountains around Nerja

Climbing out of the ravine

Further along the route will pass **La Calera del Pozuelo**, an old lime kiln (*calera*).

> There's a notice board at **La Calera del Pozuelo** with information about the production and usages of lime: the limestone rocks were gathered and burnt using firewood, the fires burning for three days and three nights. The lime was used for many purposes: to sterilize wells and fountains during pandemics; for the covering of dead bodies; as a mortar for construction; and to whitewash the houses.

The only difficult point to navigate on this route is on the approach to the **Mirador del Pozuelo**. Here the dirt track divides, the viewing point (*mirador*) on the right and the route to follow on the left. Next you need to traverse over a firebreak where the waymarkers are absent. As you descend the route narrows to a path. ▶ The path down to the ravine is very steep, over solid rock, with fixed chains to assist the climb.

> **El Saltillo bridge** was constructed exclusively to facilitate the route between Canillas de Aceituno and Sedella. It was opened in October 2020 at a cost of €630,000 – just for walkers!

Return to the **Sedella recreation area** along the same route. To call in at Sedella visitor centre, continue down to the **MA-126**, then turn left. The visitor centre is at the entrance to the village.

You are likely to hear the people on the bridge before you catch sight of it.

The Mountains around Nerja

WALK 22
Torrecilla de La Maroma

Start/Finish	Alcaucín
Distance	15km (16km if you return on the easy dirt track)
Height gain	1005m
Difficulty	5
Time	5hr 30min (same time if you return on the easy dirt track)
Getting there	Take the motorway towards Málaga, exiting at Vélez-Málaga, and going right (north) towards Vélez-Málaga and Alhama. Several kilometres after Vélez-Málaga go right, in the direction of Alhama, and then take a right again into Alcaucín. On entering the village with its welcome sign, take the road to your left that is signposted for the recreation area of El Alcázar. At a sharp left-hand turn in this road, before leaving the village, the road passes through an open area. Municipal garbage trucks park here and there may be a pile of sand for gritting the roads when they are icy. Immediately to the right off the bend in the road is Calle Carrión (///funded.swooshed.kilt). There should be ample room to park in the area of the garbage trucks and sand.
Options	Return on an easy dirt track.

A fine walk up to a promontory shoulder on La Maroma, through a pine forest, on an ancient track. The second highest mountain in the Province of Málaga is Torrecilla 1919m, which is up near Ronda. This Torrecilla (1524m) is on the western side of La Maroma, and is therefore referred to as Torrecilla de La Maroma. The hike is a decent and interesting one, through a shaded pine forest, thence up over bare rock to a fine vantage point, on an ancient purpose-made path. If you are lucky enough to be doing this walk in March, you will walk through an abundance of asphodels and rosemary.

Walk into **Calle Carrión**. Take the first lane to the left, just short of a school. On this lane there is a sign for a *sendero*. Climb the steps and follow this path. The sendero is

WALK 22 – TORRECILLA DE LA MAROMA

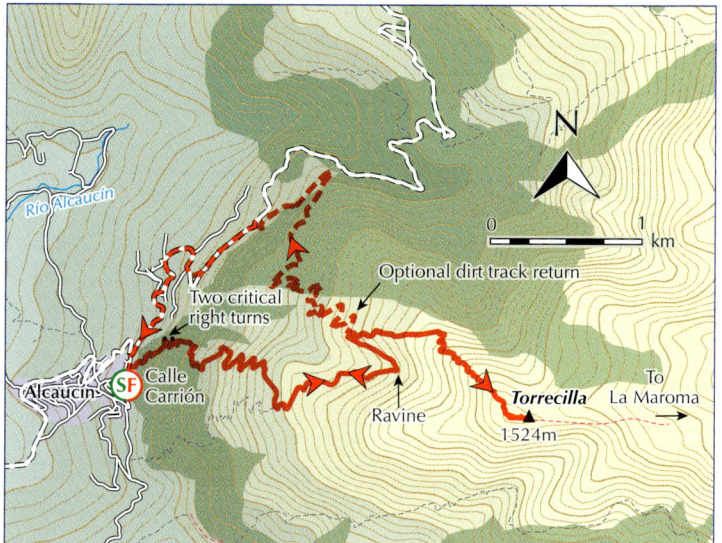

actually a walk that goes from Alcaucín to El Alcázar, but Walk 22 follows it initially.

There are two critical right-hand turns to make on the path. Follow the map and make sure you don't miss these turns. The path is over steep, stony ground.

The path zig-zags up through a pine forest. When it emerges from the forest you will be walking through rosemary and, in March, a wonderful display of asphodels.

The path eventually leads into and out of a **ravine**. The vegetation may be quite dense in the area of the ravine. The path rises to meet a dirt track (concreted in places). Do not step onto the dirt track but go right immediately before it.

The route climbs, often passing false summits, on an ancient man-made path, and out into the open over bare rock. Eventually you will come to a crest with cairns marking the summit (1524m). If you walk over the elongated summit you will see the path continuing ahead to La Maroma.

Asphodels on Torrecilla

From the summit you can look over to the pass of Zafarraya and the flat, fertile land beyond it. Below is the recreation area of El Alcázar, the starting point for Walk 17.

Retrace your steps to Alcaucín.

Optional easier return route
Retrace your steps on the initial descent. When you reach the point where the path almost touches the dirt track, if you are weary of walking over stony ground, and want to chat to your fellow walkers, and/or if you want to avoid the encroaching vegetation in the ravine and the steep stony descent in the pine forest, turn right and follow the dirt track back down to your car.

WALKS FROM THE EAST

The summit of El Cielo (Walk 23)

The first walk in this section is a very good alternative to Walk 6 to El Cielo, and its start is quite close to Nerja. It heads into the remote Valle de la Miel, the valley of honey.

The other walks explore the Valle del Río Verde, the valley of the green river, a valley that boasts a sub-tropical climate. To get there, drive east through the town of Almuñécar, then north through the villages of Jete and Otívar. The drive alone is itself worth doing, even you were never to get out of the car, for it meanders through the most spectacular landscape of deep gorges and jagged limestone ridges. Along the route are restaurants with great views serving delicious local food at remarkably low costs.

WALK 23
El Cielo from Valle de la Miel

Start/Finish	Valle de la Miel, east of Nerja
Distance	11km
Height gain	1080m
Difficulty	5
Time	6hr 30min
Getting there	Follow the road from Nerja out to Maro and proceed on the N-340 in the direction of Almería. 2.5km beyond the Maro roundabout take the road to the left. This secondary road goes under the motorway and rises steeply via zig-zags into the Valle de la Miel (valley of honey). Four kilometres along this secondary road take the minor road to the left. The start of the walk is 3km up this minor road beside a cairn, or a set of cairns, on the left-hand side of the road (///toga.debt.thumb). There is room to park two cars about 50m back towards Nerja, at the bend. Otherwise, it will be necessary to park on the side of the road.
Options	The option of a circuit may be rendered very difficult due to thick vegetation.
Note	This is not a walk for shorts, because the prickly vegetation can be difficult on the legs.

During the summer and early autumn the dirt track at the Cave of Nerja into Pinarillo is closed (see Walk 6), so that 8km must be added to the climbs of El Cielo, Almendrón and Navachica. This walk is a good alternative to the El Cielo circuit featured in Walk 6. It is shorter than Walk 6; the height gain is less; the gradient is less steep near the summit; and there will be fewer people. The disadvantages are that it is not easy to find the start, and there is very little parking there. In the past the path was ill-defined, often confusing, but in recent times the path has become quite clear and is well cairned.

Marked on the map is a possible option to make a circuit around the summit of El Cielo. However, a word of caution: it passes through an area of very thick vegetation. At time of publication this thick vegetation was almost impossible to get through, but it may be cut back in future. If the route off the El Madroño ridge does not appear well trodden and is obviously not well used, you can assume that the traverse is virtually impassable, and the circuit option can be dismissed.

The path rises through rosemary and furze, over limestone conglomerate rock. After half an hour it passes a narrow cave, on the right, that may have been used as a mine in the past. In spring you may see flowers, such as the yellow hare's ear (*Bupleurum*), or the richly pink gladiolas. After an hour of steady climbing you will reach the ruins of **Cortijo del Cornocalejo** (925m). The path continues up on the right of the *cortijo*. ▸

The peak above the cortijo is the Cabeza de Caballo, although you'll need a good imagination to decipher the shape of a horse's head.

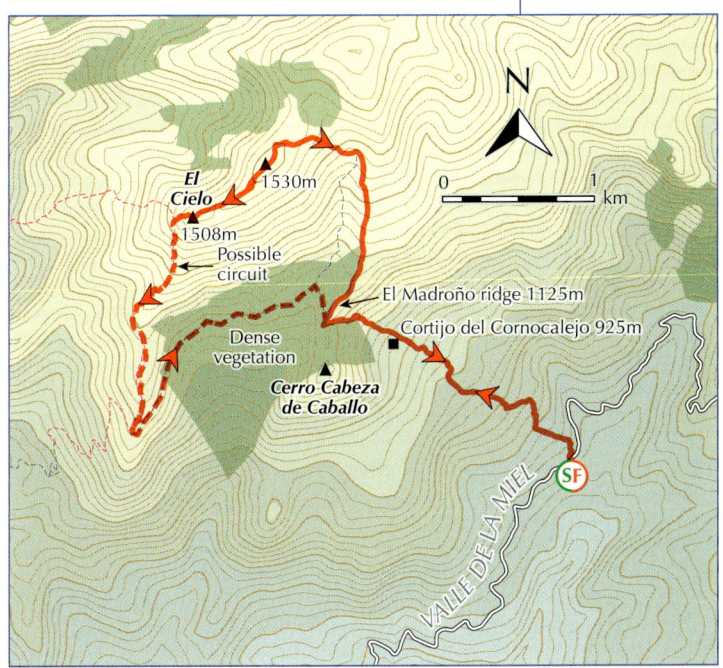

The Mountains around Nerja

The path to El Cielo from the north

The **cortijo** was once a bustling farm, harvesting olives, growing fruit and vegetables, using the *esparto* grass to make rope, herding goats and hunting boar. There was a water source (now gone dry) above the buildings.

When you reach the ridge known as **El Madroño** (1125m), you are more than halfway to your goal. From here you can see El Cielo for the first time, noting that it is not the highest point of your journey. Proceed to the right, and presently you will come to a path junction. ▶

This is the optional circuit point – examine the descending path to the left, and if it appears well used then the circuit option is likely to be passable.

The path to the summit sweeps over to the right (north) and then to the left (west). It passes through an area of burnt pine trees, where the tree remains are reminiscent of a dinosaur graveyard. You will reach an altitude of **1530m**, some 22m higher than the **El Cielo summit**, before descending to the cross.

Unless the circuit is passable and you have decided to tackle it, retrace your route back over the 1530m high point, the **El Madroño ridge** and down to the **Valle de la Miel** via the cortijo.

Optional circuit route

Descend the steep path off the summit, heading initially north immediately off the summit and then gradually west. There are multiple paths off the summit, but they all eventually lead to the one path. The steep descent zig-zags down and then swings off south over a lesser gradient. The point of the traverse back to El Madroño is not marked. To find it you must be attentive to the map. It is where there is a sharp, zig-zag, right-hand turn. The path crosses over a valley to rise up and rejoin the path on the **El Madroño ridge**.

The Mountains around Nerja

WALK 24
The Petrified Waterfall

Start/Finish	On the A-4050, 2km north of El Mirador de la Cabra Montés
Distance	11km
Height gain	410m
Difficulty	4
Time	4hr
Getting there	From Almuñécar drive north through Jete and Otívar to pass the buildings on the left that make up El Mirador de la Cabra Montés, where the road levels out. Less than 2km from the *mirador* there is a road to the left with a large entrance sign for the Sierras Tejeda, Almijara y Alhama. Park here (///chiefly.gorging.metallic). The dirt track on the left is the return path.
Options	This walk and Walk 25 to the summit of Lopera could both be done in a day. Bring a swimsuit for a dip in a rock pool.

This short route takes you on an adventure into the secluded and breathtaking valley of the Río Verde to visit a very pretty and unusual waterfall, explore an interesting limestone cave and have lunch beside a lake. The drive up through the mountains is spectacular too.

The circular walk descends, very steeply in places, from the main road down to the waterfall and returns along a dirt track back to the main road. Part of the return route involves a narrow path through shrubbery. But, aside from these minor difficulties, this walk is highly recommended. The actual time walking will be much shorter than the overall time, as you will be stopping regularly to look at and photograph the many vistas.

From the **park entrance**, walk 2km along the main road until you see the waymarker on your left. The narrow path leads from the main road on an undulating course around the mountain of **Cerro Martos**. Very soon you are deep into the wilderness of the valley of the **Río Verde**,

WALK 24 – THE PETRIFIED WATERFALL

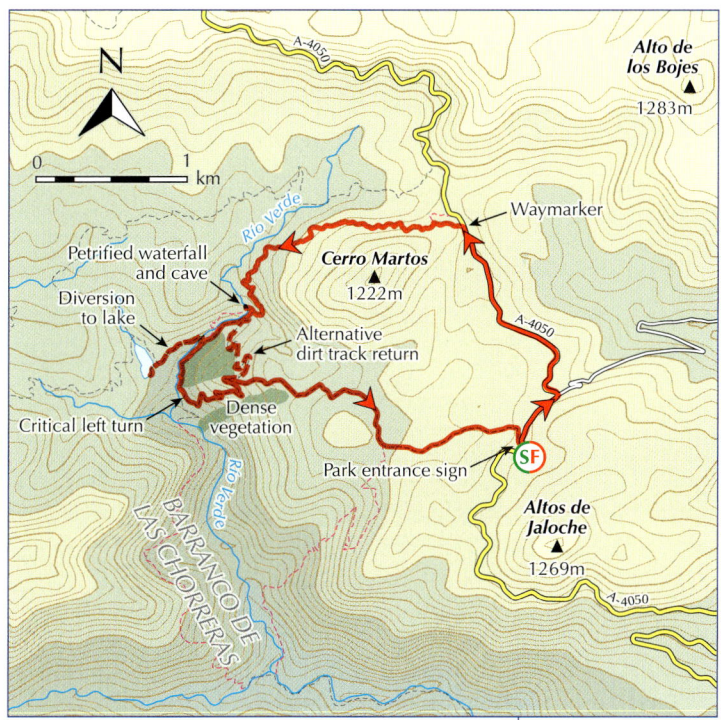

walking through pines and stunted junipers. The jagged columns of white limestone dominate the landscape.

In less than an hour make a steep descent, aided by ropes in places and handrails over concreted steps elsewhere. Before reaching the bottom you will be able to hear the waterfall and soon after you'll catch your first glimpse of it. However, at the bottom of the steep descent there is a track on your right. A few metres along that track is a limestone cave where water seeping from the roof has produced some wonderful features in the walls. You will not need a head torch, but the pools in the far reaches of the cave are ankle deep. ▶

At the base of the waterfall, in the shade of the trees, there is a lovely shallow pool with cool water. You could picnic here or wait until you get to the lake.

THE MOUNTAINS AROUND NERJA

The petrified waterfall

The **waterfall** was created by the trunks of trees becoming coated in the lime chemicals of the water. About 30 years ago the tree trunks that had been felled were being brought down the river. They were manoeuvred over the waterfall and left to stand there. Over the years the lime minerals in the water covered the trunks and formed a thick coating.

Leaving the waterfall and going west you will come to a dirt-track road. ◄ At the dirt track turn right and, 200m further along, a waymarked path will appear on

If you are tired, turn left at the track to curtail the walk and return to your car. But you will miss out on some wonderful scenery.

the left. This is your return route. However, if you continue along the track for another 300m you will come to a lake, which is a pleasant, alternative place to have lunch.

Retrace your steps to the waymarked track and you will come down into the heart of the **Río Verde** (green river). It is aptly named, for the vegetation along the river is decidedly green. ▶

Next you need to be careful. The dirt track leads deep into the sierra. Within 1km of where you joined this track, or a few hundred metres from the rock pools, there is a narrow path to the left. There should be cairns here marking this **critical left turn**. This narrow path through **dense vegetation** zig-zags up to a wide dirt track, where you turn right, and make the 3km easy trek back to the **park entrance**.

If the weather is hot there are rock pools here to cool off in. After periods of rain, water gushes over a 50m-high waterfall into the river.

Descent into the valley of the Río Verde

The Mountains around Nerja

WALK 25
Lopera

Start/Finish	On the A-4050, 8km north of El Mirador de la Cabra Montés
Distance	8.7km
Height gain	275m
Difficulty	1
Time	3hr
Getting there	From Almuñécar you need the road to Jete (pronounced 'hetay') and Otívar, which is in the opposite direction to the beach. Coming from Nerja, you cannot turn left onto this road, but must first turn right and then cross the main road. This minor road, the A-4050, climbs out of town, passes under the motorway (N-340) and continues to climb higher. Driving north through Jete and Otívar you will pass the buildings on the left that make up El Mirador de la Cabra Montés (lookout point for the mountain goat). Continue for 8km beyond the *mirador*, passing through a short tunnel, to arrive at the restaurant Mesón Los Prados (the house of the meadows) on the left-hand side of the road (///imprisoned.nurturing.married).
Options	This could be combined, with Walk 24 to the Petrified Waterfall, into a single day's walk.

It is a rarity to be able to walk for just an hour and reach the summit of the highest mountain in an area and to experience its 360-degree vista. But you can with Lopera (1485m), and the ascent is easy.

It is also rare to walk in Spain through meadows and wheat fields, passing hawthorn and deciduous oak trees, with grasses and flowers that would be common in Ireland and the British Isles.

After parking at the restaurant **Mesón Los Prados**, walk back along the A-4050 towards Otívar for 700m. It is less than 3km from the main road to the summit of Lopera.

WALK 25 – LOPERA

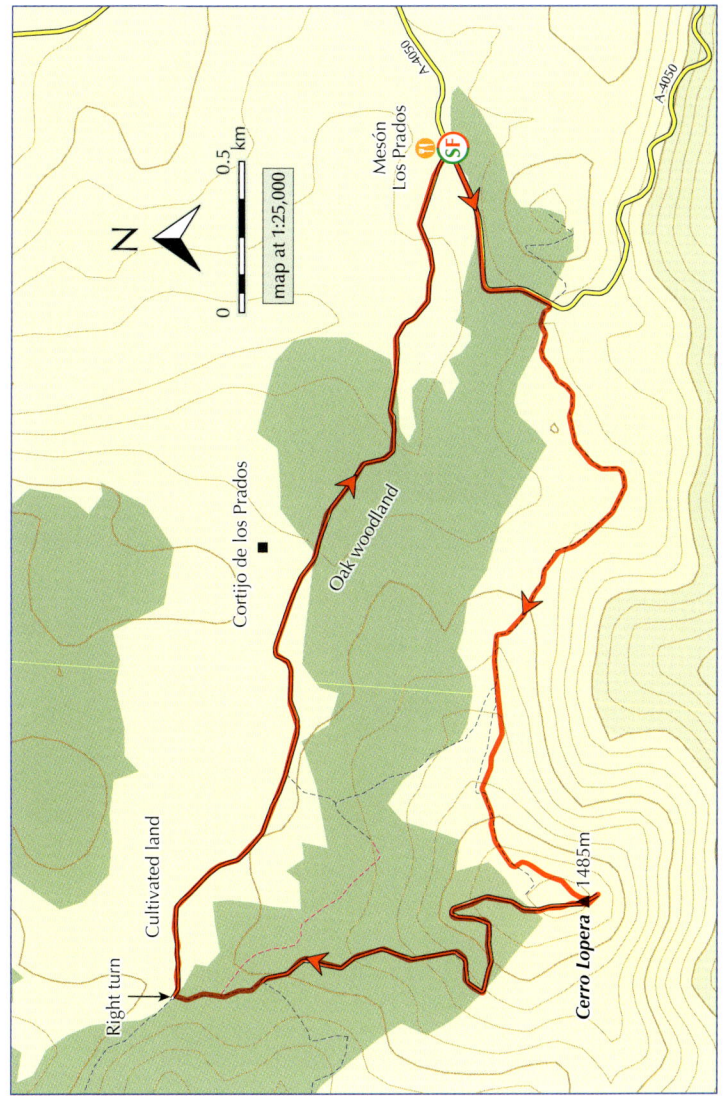

Lopera summit

The summit of Cerro Lopera is capped by a meteorological observatory, whose primary purpose is to watch over the sierra for the outbreak of fires.

Turn right off the road and follow the waymarkers along a wide firebreak to the summit. For the entire approach your objective is clearly in view. ◂

From the **summit of Cerro Lopera** there is a fine panoramic view. To the east is the Sierra Nevada – Lopera is the nearest summit in these mountains to the Sierra Nevada. The orientation table below the observatory picks out the other peaks to the south and west. Sadly, there is no route from here to the summit of Navachica – most of the land between Lopera and Navachica is in private ownership.

The waymarks only go to the summit of the mountain. The return walk is along unwaymarked dirt tracks. Walk away from the summit in a northerly direction, along a wide dirt track that descends directly north. Now the route is through pines on either side.

WALK 25 – LOPERA

After 2km a road joins from the left and the signs indicate that the land to the left is private. So, continue northwards to a sharp bend in the road where another path joins from the left. This is the area of the *prados* (meadows) – fields that have been cultivated for grain for centuries. Follow the road to the right, with hawthorn trees close by, all the way down to the restaurant. Further on, beyond the large farm building, the walk goes through **woodland of deciduous oaks**. ▶

This area is very popular at weekends with families coming to picnic and people walking and pony trekking.

The large farm building is called **Cortijo de los Prados**, the farmhouse of the meadows, and the area around it is Huerto Alegre, the happy kitchen gardens. The establishment is a school for farm husbandry.

The dirt track runs all the way to the main road and the **Mesón Los Prados**, which may be quite full at weekends. The food is good, the servings are generous, and the price is remarkably cheap.

Hawthorn tree

WALKS FROM THE NORTH

The Ventas de Zafarraya pass with Pico del Puerto on the right

To the north of the mountains of Nerja the land is elevated, being in excess of 900m. The area from Ventas de Zafarraya over to Alhama de Granada is a virtual flat plateau of fertile land that receives more rainfall than the coast.

Ventas de Zafarraya is a spectacular pass (*boquete* or *puerto*) through the Sierra Tejeda mountains that affords passage into the great plains of the northern Axarquía. The pass is at an elevation of 900m. During the time of the Phoenicians the Río Vélez was navigable up to Vélez-Málaga. This allowed invaders to come in from the sea and the route up through the Zafarraya pass provided good access to Granada.

To do the walks in Alhama de Granada, La Maroma from Alcacería, or Malascamas, you will go through the pass at Ventas de Zafarraya. But, if you are not disposed to long walks and/or long drives, then you should at least come up to experience the wonderful scenery of the pass. The next two short walks, 26 and 27, both start at the same point and both offer stunning views. These two walks can be completed, one after the other, inside a short day.

In the early part of the last century there was a narrow-gauge steam railway that connected the villages of La Viñuela, Periana and Zafarraya to Vélez-Málaga and Torre del Mar. The railway was to eventually connect Granada to the sea, but in 1928 the plans were abandoned.

WALK 26
Pico del Puerto

Start/Finish	Parking area just after the pass, Ventas de Zafarraya
Distance	6km
Height gain	355m
Difficulty	4 (but see Options, below)
Time	3hr
Getting there	Drive from Nerja towards Málaga, and take the exit for Vélez-Málaga and Torre del Mar. Turn right and drive up, passing Vélez-Málaga and following the directions for Alhama de Granada. The walk begins at a parking area immediately on the left after going through the pass and before entering the village. Turn sharp left after the overhead bridge and take the steep road that leads up to a viewing area. Park here (///prototype.fearful.honest).
Options	The difficulty factor can be reduced to 2 by ascending and descending the same (return) 'Easier option' (detailed below). Walks 26 and 27 can be combined, with lunch at the pass, to make a full day's walk.
Note	Within a classical col of these proportions the wind speeds can be high and the temperature cold. Clouds very often tend to engulf these mountains.

The scenery is amazing up here. This walk will take you under the Tajo de la Cuna, to circle and climb up to Pico del Puerto, the highest point in this area at 1225m. You may see peregrine falcons on this walk.

On the opposite side of the road, back under the bridge and below the pass is the start of the walk. Note that this is initially over private land. The walk sets off south-east on a wide dirt track, but presently a boulder blocks the way and you have to negotiate a narrow path where the vegetation gradually makes walking a little more difficult. The views over the countryside are stunning, and there are many caves and holes through the mountain. ▶

> The second cliff face you pass has caves where peregrine falcons nest; you might see them soaring overhead or calling warnings of intruders.

THE MOUNTAINS AROUND NERJA

Under the falcon cliff

After two zig-zags the **cut-out path** comes to an end. From here to the summit you will require some experience at steep climbing over unmarked ground. You can climb directly northeast towards the summit, getting there by scrambling over the bare rock, or you can climb further to the north where you will meet a path that leads to the summit.

At the summit of **Pico del Puerto** there are two *miradores* (viewpoints) with signs informing that this walk is known as the *Sendero de la Cuna* (the path of the cradle).

Waymarker posts will guide you back to the start, initially heading east to descend from the summit. ▶ The descent is generally gentle, along a grassy path down to the village of **Ventas de Zafarraya**, where you turn left, then walk over the bridge to the car park (following the tracks of the narrow-gauge railway).

Near the top of the mountain you will circle the cradle (land protected on all sides from the wind) that gives this walk its name.

Easier option

To reduce the difficulty of this walk, cross the bridge after leaving the car park and follow the tracks of the narrow-gauge railway. Presently you will come to a sign that says Sendero de la Cuna. Turn right and the waymarker posts will take you to the summit. Return the same way.

The cradle near the summit of Pico del Puerto

THE MOUNTAINS AROUND NERJA

WALK 27
The hole in the mountain

Start/Finish	Parking area just after the pass, Ventas de Zafarraya
Distance	3km
Height gain	265m
Difficulty	3
Time	1hr 30min
Getting there	Drive from Nerja towards Málaga, and take the exit for Vélez-Málaga and Torre del Mar. Turn right and drive up, passing Vélez-Málaga and following the directions for Alhama de Granada. The walk begins at a parking area immediately on the left after going through the pass and before entering the village. Turn sharp left after the overhead bridge and take the steep road that leads up to a viewing area. Park here (///fads.sparklers.measurement).
Options	Walks 26 and 27 can be combined, with lunch at the pass, to make a full day's walk.

This is a waymarked walk with spectacular views that goes into the Sierra Alhama, offering the chance to look through the hole in the mountain.

The path leads off beside the *sendero* information sign (elevation 923m). This is a tough little climb. It will be half an hour before you arrive at the first viewing point, **Mirador de los Pradillos**, and a further 20 minutes or so before you reach the summit.

> The **limestone** forms tall chimneys on this exposed path. These limestones are of Jurassic origin, much younger than the limestones of La Maroma or Navachica.

Near the summit you will have to clamber over bare rock and wonder what is before you. And then you see

WALK 27 – THE HOLE IN THE MOUNTAIN

it – the enormous cave. As you descend for a closer look you realise that it is a massive **hole through the mountain**.

From the summit, at 1188m, you have a panoramic view: southwards to the sea; westwards to the Viñuela reservoir and beyond to the Mountains of Málaga; eastwards to the hulk of La Maroma; and northwards to the fertile plains of Alhama de Granada.

Be careful to avoid sliding on the stony path as you descend. Admire the very prickly, yet delicate, Andalucían thistles on the side of the path.

Looking through the hole in the mountain

WARNING

Some maps indicate a path that gives the option of making this walk into a circuit, by continuing to the west and then descending to the north. There is no path, no route, this way. The map is incorrect. The vegetation and the rock profile make this route impassable.

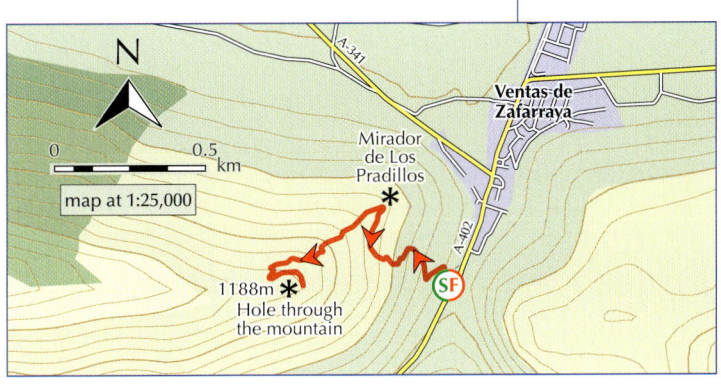

WALK 28
Malascamas via Barranco de Malinfierno

Start/Finish	Parque Natural sign beyond La Platilla quarry
Distance	17.5km
Height gain	865m
Difficulty	6
Time	7hr
Getting there	Drive from Alcaicería towards Alhama de Granada. Just before the town of Alhama take the road to the right for Jatar and Arenas del Rey. Pass by a reservoir and, 5.5km further on, take the paved road to the right, signposted Almacén; this road leads to a large farming area and a quarry (at time of publication, signposted La Platilla). After the quarry the road turns into a dirt track; at the first fork take the left-hand option, following the main track; drive through farms and past houses and, 2.5km past the last entry to the quarry, you will reach a Parque Natural sign on the left. Turn left onto a dirt track and proceed to a gate. Park here (///celebrities.hubs.refused).
Options	There is an extension at the start of the route to avoid walking over private land. Hostelries at Alcaicería and the Alhama reservoir are good, convenient places to spend the night.

This classic walk over an old *camino* to the source of the Río Alhama – and the very heart of the mountains – has all the ingredients for a good day's hike: good length, a little scrambling, an interesting route through the *barranco*, and arrival at a pointed peak. Once you have negotiated the start, the route is relatively straightforward and easy to follow. You reach Malascamas via a grassy col just under the summit. You can enjoy all the views from this col; however, if you want to bag the summit there is a difficult passage over loose scree and a scramble to the top.

At 1793m Malascamas (bad beds) is the highest of the intermediate group of mountains between La Maroma and Cerro de la Chapa. It cannot be seen from Nerja. Like La Maroma, it is remote, being nearly 9km from a place where a car can travel to and considerably further away from a paved road. Malascamas can also be approached from the south from La Fábrica de la Luz (Walk 14), from Robledal (Walk 31), and even via the SUV drive featured in Walk 15.

Although the signs on the gate at the start of the walk say that the land is private, nobody lives here and there are no buildings – just a few olive trees. ▶ All maps show that the 'private land' is, in fact, part of the Parque Natural. You can proceed past the gate (at time of publication, there was no fence to cross – just step around the gate), climb to reach a second gate and step over the fence into the Parque Natural.

The road (what is left of it) through the Barranco Malinfierno was obviously an established ancient route, and is most likely a public right of way.

Optional diversion around private land
If you are reluctant to pass the 'private' sign, you can proceed on the dirt track left of the gate and follow the alternative route shown on the map, which will add one hour to the journey each way.

Main route
In spite of its name, **Barranco de Malinfierno** (ravine of bad hell) is actually a very pleasant route to walk. It is a 4km trek following the river. In the mornings the barranco is shaded from the sun. Peaks will come into view but none of them is Malascamas – you don't get your first glimpse until after you've emerged from the ravine.

> This used to be a proper path that a cart could negotiate (you will see the remains of old culverts), but **floods** have destroyed it in a number of places. The most severe flood in the past few decades occurred in September 2007 when over 200mm of rain fell within 24 hours.

The path diverts away from the river in places, but eventually returns. Two-thirds of the way into the barranco the brown limestone is prone to erosion and the

THE MOUNTAINS AROUND NERJA

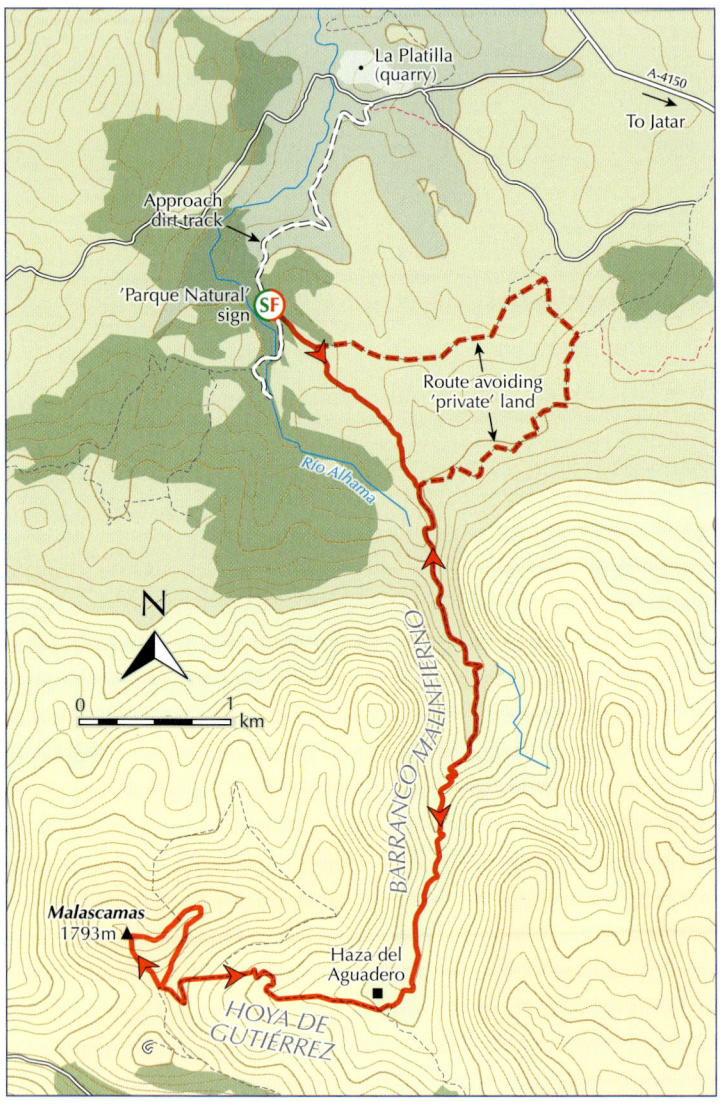

river has caused the rock to collapse. Eventually the path arrives at a virtual oasis in the wilderness, **Haza del Aguadero**. ▶ This is the source of the Río Alhama, the river that cuts through the gorge of Alhama, travels north collecting tributaries and expands to a mighty river before discharging into the great lake at Iznájar.

From the farm the mountains appear to form a long ridgeline stretching away to the west. The peak at the far end of this ridge is Malascamas.

> **Haza del Aguadero**, now sadly dilapidated, is a pleasant place to rest. This extensive farm was fully working until the great 2007 flood. With its access severed, the flood sounded the death knell for the farm. Now the only inhabitant is a shepherd who manages a herd of goats. The crocuses that are common in northern Europe in the spring bloom here in early spring and again in the autumn. In February and early March the almond trees are in full bloom.

Entry to the Barranco de Malinfierno

At Haza del Aguadero the direction changes to due west and follows a dirt track that zigzags into the mountains. This valley is **Hoya de Gutiérrez**. The rise is gradual. After 2km ignore the path on the right and continue to a grassy col at 1651m.

> From **the col** La Maroma can be seen in all its splendour. Above the col to the right of La Maroma is the trigonometric station on the summit of Malascamas (1793m).

There is no easy path to the summit of **Malascamas**. Off the dirt track and swinging away to the right of the col there is the semblance of a goat track. This leads to the summit from the rear.

THE MOUNTAINS AROUND NERJA

The remains of the farm at Haza del Aguadero

The alternative is to opt for a direct climb. The best option is to go up the steep way, negotiating your way through sparse vegetation over loose scree and bare rock, and then come down on the goat track.

The top of the ridge is a series of jagged **limestone outcrops**. Perhaps this is where the name 'bad beds' comes from. From the summit a distinct path can be seen proceeding from the grassy col all the way over and up La Maroma (see Walk 15).

Return to the start of the walk via the same route; the journey can be shortened by going off track to bypass the many hairpins.

WALK 29
The Gorge of Alhama de Granada

Start/Finish	Tourist office beside the town hall, Alhama de Granada
Distance	6km
Height gain	110m
Difficulty	1
Time	2hr 30min
Getting there	Alhama de Granada is 70km from Nerja. Drive along the motorway towards Malagá; turn off at Vélez-Málaga; take the A-402 to go north through the mountain pass, following the signs for Alhama de Granada (///principally.exert.pickups).
Options	Return back up through the town instead of along the road opposite the gorge. Visit the hot springs of Alhama afterwards (by car).

'One of the unsung gems of the Granada Province' is how the *Rough Guide to Andalucía* refers to Alhama de Granada. The town is at an elevation of 1000m and its population has been dwindling for a number of decades. It is perched over a gorge and the route begins by walking through this gorge and then returns on the opposite cliff top.

This route is waymarked as the *Sendero de Termalismo*.

The **tourist office** provides free maps of the town and brochures of the attractions in the area. Housed in a nearby building is a collection of old photographs showing the lives of local people over the years.

Go to the left of the **tourist office** and around to the rear to look down into the gorge, and take the second set of steps. At the bottom of the steps are the ruins of one of the five **flour mills** of Alhama, but going further down to explore them is not very interesting. So, turn to the right and proceed along under the daunting cliff. ▶

En route watch out for the *pilas de lavar*, stones shaped to assist in the washing of clothes.

THE MOUNTAINS AROUND NERJA

Miocene sandstone

These horizontally bedded **Miocene sandstones** are only 15 million years old, so they post-date the mountain-building era of southern Andalucía. Old farm buildings and a 16th-century church have been cut into the soft rock.

Further along a noticeboard tells the legend of The Leap of the Horse – do take the time to climb up onto the boulder to examine the hoof marks that the legendary horse made when it landed.

For an alternative return route, turn right and go back along the main road, walking into town on a path above the gorge.

Eventually the path reaches and crosses a **wooden bridge** and goes out to the main road. Turn left and walk along the road to a shaded area, where there is a **bird-watcher's hide** that overlooks the reservoir. ◄ Across the main road from the hide there is a fine **restaurant** very suitable for lunch or a coffee.

WALK 29 – THE GORGE OF ALHAMA DE GRANADA

Take the paved road that goes left (there is a signpost for the Sendero de Termalismo). This is a little-used road that climbs gently along the far side of the gorge. ▶ Halfway along the road there is a *mirador*, a **viewing point** that looks down into the gorge and over to the town. This is a good spot for a rest and photographs.

Continue along the road and presently follow a sign that points left, down into the gorge again. After the path goes through a **pass in the rocks** take the first path on the right, which climbs up steep steps to emerge at the **dungeons**.

In February, the almond trees along this road are in full bloom.

THE MOUNTAINS AROUND NERJA

Bienvenidos (welcome) to Alhama

The so-called **dungeons** are large vaulted structures that were originally created by the Moors for grain storage, but they were also used for other purposes, such as the incarceration of prisoners during the Civil War.

Beyond the dungeons there is a narrow lane that leads up to one of Alhama's longest streets. **Calle Llana** connects a square at the eastern end of town to Plaza Santiago at the western end. Turn left to return to the tourist office.

ALHAMA'S HOT SPRINGS

The name Alhama comes from the Arabic Al Hammam, which means hot bath. If you drive through the town in the direction of Granada, there are natural hot springs just outside Alhama on the A-402. Turn left off the road, following signs for Balneario. Here you may go into the hotel and pay for a hot, outdoor bath, or use the small pools to the side of the hotel where bathing is free. En route to the hot springs there is a Roman bridge on the right.

WALK 30
La Resinera

Start/Finish	La Resinera Interpretive Centre, near Fornes
Distance	11km
Height gain	235m
Difficulty	1
Time	3hr
Getting there	From Arenas del Rey head in the direction of the village of Fornes, but just short of the village follow the sign for La Resinera (///hairspray.turns.scissors).
Options	Explore the village of Fornes, visit the interpretive centre and learn about the resin industry of former times.
Note	Although the difficulty is rated as 1, it is advisable to bring sticks and wear boots rather than shoes, because the ground underfoot on the descent is rough, and you will need to cross a stream.

This is a circular half-day route through peaceful countryside with a high chance of seeing some red deer and with marvellous view from the summit. The walk is waymarked but the waymarkers are few and far between; to add to the confusion, for a brief initial period, the route follows the GR7.

La Resinera is one of two interpretive centres in the Parque Natural – the other is in Sedella. In the centre, which is housed in a former church building, there are visual displays of the local plants and wildlife and interactive displays about the local history and way of life. A visit is highly recommended (open Fri–Sun 9.30am–2.30pm).

To the left of the **interpretive centre**, take the dirt-track road that drops down to the river. This is a popular picnic spot where people come to bathe in the Río Cacín. Cross the bridge and proceed out into the country. ▶

Pass the ruin of a former *calera* (limestone kiln). Presently the road meets the river again, at a concrete ford where the water may be a few centimetres deep. At a fork in the dirt track, follow the sign for Mesa de Fornes,

The walk is under cliffs of soft sandstone. These sandstones are young in geological terms, being of Quaternary age ('only' 2.5 million years old).

Picnic area at La Resinera

leaving the GR7 walk. Next comes a steady but long climb to the flat land at the summit.

Mesa de Fornes, the Table of Fornes (1080m), is a flat promontory area, with cliffs on three sides and a trigonometry point, high and directly in front. To the left of it are the ruins of buildings believed to have been built by the Phoenicians. To the right is the path, marked with white-painted stones.

Follow the path round to the viewing point and continue round the top of the cliff. The path then turns right and descends, over rough ground, in the direction of **Fornes**. Just as the path touches the outskirts of the village there is a sharp turn – take this road to the left.

The waymarkers, if you can spot them, guide you past housing and farms onto a narrow path that runs alongside an irrigation channel. Eventually that path emerges onto the concrete road to La Resinera, where you turn left.

THE RESIN INDUSTRY

When a pine tree is cut it oozes resin, the sticky liquid that assists in healing the tree's wound. In the late 19th and 20th centuries this resin was a commercial product with many uses. Pine trees were cut in regular patterns and cups were affixed to catch the oozing resin. At the height of resin production many thousands of people were employed in the industry. Sierra Tejeda takes its name from the word *tejo*, meaning yew and, before the resin industry began to flourish, all the yew trees were cut down to make way for pines. The yews were also considered poisonous to livestock.

WALK 30 – LA RESINERA

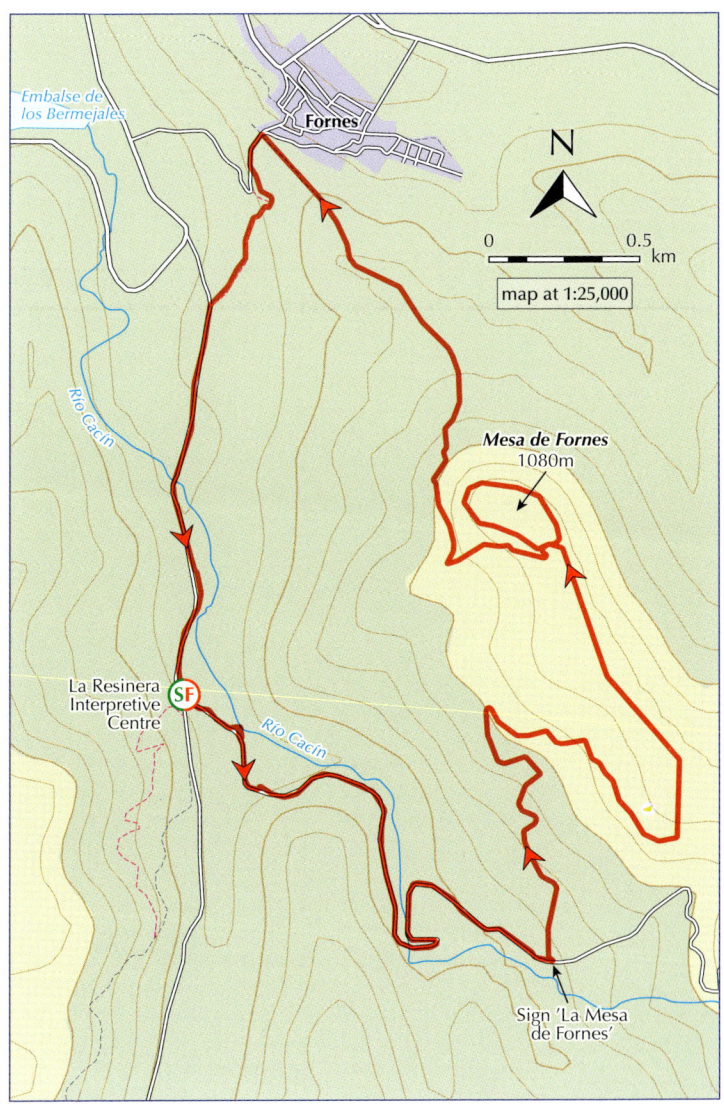

149

The Mountains around Nerja

WALK 31
Malascamas from Robledal

Start/Finish	Robledal
Distance	16km
Height gain	955m
Difficulty	5
Time	6hr 30min
Getting there	This walk starts south of Alcaicería at the same place as Walk 19, Robledal. Come off the motorway at Vélez-Málaga and head north in the direction of Alhama de Granada and Zafarraya. The road heads through Ventas de Zafarraya, a natural pass in the Sierra Tejeda. Above Zafarraya, on the road to Alhama de Granada, drive over an elevated plateau of fertile farmland. At a height of 950m, this plateau enjoys considerably more rainfall than the lands below. Ten kilometres from Zafarraya you will reach the locality of Alcaicería. To the right of a hotel on the road, take the dirt track in the direction of Cortijo de Robledal (///stacks.zygotes.indexes).

Malascamas is the most remote of the mountains in the Parque Natural, and this is a walk in wild country where you are unlikely to meet anyone. It is possible to make the SUV drive described in Walk 15, in which case it would be a very short distance to the mountain. Otherwise this is the shortest route to Malascamas. It has the disadvantage that there is no defined path for some of the walk, so you need to navigate your own route.

After parking at the **Robledal recreation area**, walk back up the road to the first junction. Turn right in the direction of **Cerezal Alto**. A kilometre and a half down this rough dirt track, through pine woods, you will cross a stream. Immediately afterwards there is a **gateway** on your right. Go through the gate and follow the dirt track – it goes to a modern house that has been built over an old country inn, **Venta Palma**.

WALK 31 – MALASCAMAS FROM ROBLEDAL

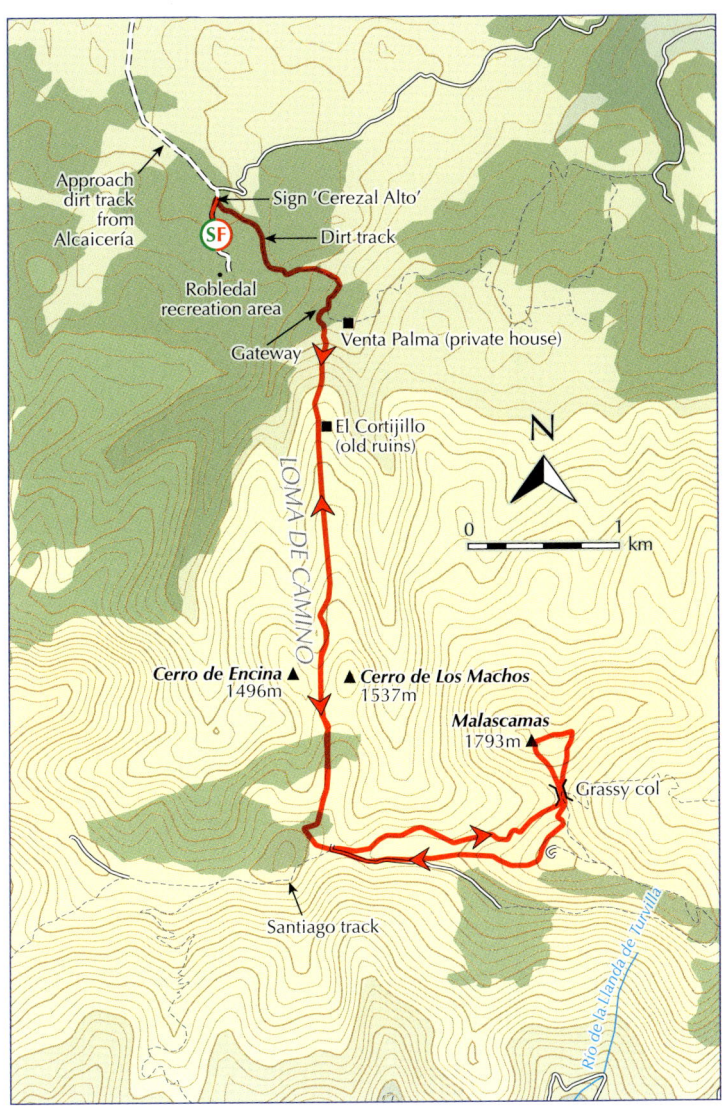

151

THE MOUNTAINS AROUND NERJA

The path through the valley of Loma de Camino

Although there is a sign (old and illegible) on the gateway saying the land is private, it is within the Parque Natural, which means it is **free to roam**. In any case, there is never anyone around to challenge you and, as long as you close the gate, there should be no problem.

Keep a close eye on your mobile map to ensure you are more or less on the route; with a bit of luck you may spot helpful cairns.

Walk up the rise to join a farm road and proceed generally in a southerly direction. Farm animals have created multiple tracks over the land, so there is no defined path. ◀ After several kilometres, when you come over a crest, you will see the path clearly through the valley ahead. This is **Loma de Camino**. On the right is Cerro de Encina (1496m) and on the left Cerro de Los Machos (1537m).

Proceed through the valley and, as you emerge on the other side, Malascamas will come into view on your left. Carry straight on, rising to the south, until you meet and join the dirt track that crosses the sierra in an east–west direction. This track, sometimes known as the **Santiago**

WALK 31 – MALASCAMAS FROM ROBLEDAL

road, is at an elevation of 1600m. Unfortunately, having climbed this far, the route now descends before reaching the **grassy col** that is at the base of the **summit of Malascamas**. The final climb may be a direct ascent to the plinthed summit. You may find it easier to climb bare rock, rather than slide on loose scree. The peaked summit, at 1793m, gives a sense of having arrived. To the west is the massive hulk of La Maroma (2069m).

Rather than going down the steep route you came up, it will be safer to veer off to the east. This reasonably well-defined route passes over bare rock to the end of the ridge, where it turns to the right (south) and comes back down to the **grassy col**.

The only return option is to retrace your steps to Robledal recreation area. Follow the obvious path up to and along the **Santiago track**, before turning right and heading back northwards through **Loma de Camino**. ▶ Before the descent towards Venta Palma you might spot the ruins of a farm building. This is **El Cortijillo**.

The first view of Malascamas after emerging from Loma de Camino

The return journey may not be as difficult to follow as the ascent, and it may be easier to spot cairns.

CISNE

Cisne's two prongs

There are other mountains and then there is Cisne. This is the most difficult of the mountains around Nerja. Often referred to as the K2 of Andalucía, it is a mere 1483m in height, but to climb it requires particular mountaineering skills. The difficulty rating of 10 is well merited – to summit Cisne involves a long walk in and out, scrambling over precipitous rock, manoeuvring through loose, steep scree and climbing the last 700m in under 3km.

WALK 32
Cisne from El Acebuchal

Start/Finish	El Acebuchal
Distance	16km (19km if you return via the high-level track instead of the ravine)
Height gain	1150m
Difficulty	10
Time	8hr
Getting there	Passing through Frigiliana on the road towards Torrox, there is a sign at 3.5km indicating El Acebuchal to the right. After a further 2.5km the road reaches the village. Park at a ravine on the right just short of El Acebuchal (/// expectation.tugs.bamboos).
Options	Instead of returning to El Acebuchal via the ravine you could return along the high-level dirt track. This option is 3km longer (each way) but it includes a fine view down over the village. With a 4WD vehicle you could drive all the way to the base of the mountain by road. To do this, turn off along a dirt track on the right 1km before the village.
Warning	This route involves precipitous sections over bare rock that must be negotiated with care, particularly on the descent from the summit.

A tough, rugged mountain, Cisne presents great challenges to the mountaineer. Perhaps you can imagine that from the air, each of the humps of its summits resemble the shoulders of a swan (*cisne* means swan in English). From Nerja the mountain is the hulk on the opposite side of the valley to Lucero, appearing to have a sheer vertical side and a rounded ridge for its summit. It will take two hours to walk to the base of the mountain. To climb it, have lunch and descend is another four hours, and the return to El Acebuchal will take a further two hours, so be prepared for a long day.

Resistance to the Franco regime continued in some parts of Andalucía for many years after the Civil War ended. The Maquis found sanctuary in the mountain villages and settlements. Indeed it was as late as 1948 that the Guardia Civil cleared **El Acebuchal** and destroyed the village. The name of the village comes from *acebuche*, meaning the wild olive tree. With the aid of grants from the government of Andalucía, the village has now been almost fully restored.

Follow the ravine to its end, ignoring a steep path on the right that rises out of it 2km from the start. Emerge onto one of two dirt tracks, turning right onto the one that goes north. ◄ A short distance later, turn left at a junction.

> It is important to remember this junction on the way back – it is easy to walk past it.

Further along the track, you will reach the ruin of **Venta Cebollero**. Take the track to the right immediately beyond this building. Ignoring the next track to the right, continue up a wide ravine to re-join the main dirt track just short of **Collado Blanquilla**. Here the first view of Cisne emerges ahead, but unfortunately the walk loses elevation after this before starting the final climb.

After 1km the dirt-track road reaches a road junction. Take the road to the right signposted Vereda del Puerto de los Umbrales. Walking down the dirt track, a path can be seen crossing the base of Cisne, which goes to the col known as Puerto de los Umbrales. Do not take this; keep following the dirt track.

Presently the road comes to a **reservoir** over a river. ◄ Following the main dirt track that passes the reservoir, cross the river a second time and walk up a concrete road.

> This is the Río Higuerón that passes to the side of Frigiliana and joins the Río Chillar just outside of Nerja.

The start of the track up Cisne is well marked. Indeed, the route to the summit is clearly marked via small cairns and coloured spots.

> An alternative, **direct approach to the summit** is marked on the map. Although more straightforward than the recommended route, there are no clear cairns to show the start, it is not well marked and it is too steep as a descent. The ascent route described below, partly over precipitous bare rock, is recommended so that you are acquainted with it as a descent.

WALK 32 – CISNE FROM EL ACEBUCHAL

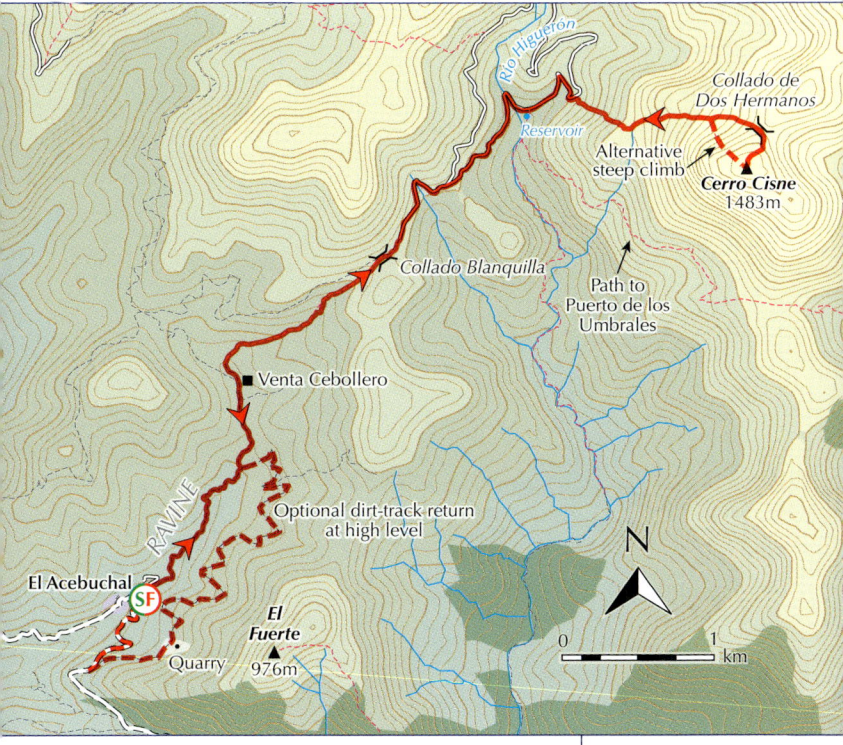

The track is narrow and steep. At 1000m you can take a breather at a col, and then another at 1200m, before the path arrives at a third col on the north side of the summit. This is **Collado de Dos Hermanos** (col of two brothers).

The path now traverses under the cliff on the eastern side of the peak to circle around behind it. At one point you will have to climb over bare rock. Negotiating the bare rock into the gully is precipitous and must be carried out with care. **This is the most dangerous part of the climb; if you or anyone with you are inexperienced, consider roping up for safety.** ▶

There is a cave on the right of the gully that would be a welcome shelter should the weather take a turn for the worse.

Cisne's final climb

From the summit there is a good view down over Frigiliana to Nerja and the coast. A look back at Lucero clearly shows the lookout structure on its summit.

Emerge onto the flat area at the top of the gully with a sigh of relief!

Cerro Cisne appears to have three summits, set out in a triangle. The one straight ahead and slightly to the left is the highest point (1483m) and can be reached by an easy scramble over rock. ◀

The mountaineer's rule that the descent should be handled with more care than the ascent is very appropriate on Cisne. The scree will slide under your boots; particular care is required when making the transition from the gully to the path; below this it is of paramount importance to watch carefully for the little cairns. There is one particular gully on the descent that it is essential to leave at the right point – if you follow it all the way down you will have to climb back because there is no exit below (apart from a 4m vertical drop).

Perspiration can be washed off in the river at the base before starting the long trudge back to El Acebuchal. After passing **Venta Cebollero** watch out for the entry into the ravine. If you miss it, the return route along the dirt track provides a fine aerial view of **El Acebuchal**.

APPENDIX A
List of peaks by altitude

The following is a list of the peaks in order of altitude – the 55 'Munros' (summits over 914m) in the mountains around Nerja that are located within the Parque Natural de Sierras Tejeda, Almijara y Alhama. Where there are summits in close proximity to each other or summits that follow a ridge, only the highest point is included here. There are many unnamed peaks that have not been included.

1	La Maroma	2069m
2	Navachica	1831m
3	Selladero	1829m
4	Tojo Fuerte	1826m
5	La Chapa	1818m
6	Malascamas	1793m
7	La Majada del Arce	1789m
8	Lucero	1779m
9	Albucaz	1726m
10	Cabañeros	1716m
11	La Venta Panaderos	1687m
12	Piedra Sillada	1678m
13	Mota	1649m
14	Santiago	1645m
15	La Cadena	1645m
16	Los Llanos	1644m
17	Tajadillas Oscuras	1642m
18	Tacita de Plata	1639m
19	Alto de los Buitres	1615m
20	Los Majanos	1605m
21	Los Corrales	1596m
22	Tajo del Sol	1550m
23	Los Machos	1537m
24	Cenacho	1527m
25	Peñón Rodado	1522m
26	Loma la Chaparral	1516m
27	Tajo de Almendrón	1515m
28	El Fuerte (nr Nerja)	1509m
29	El Cielo	1508m
30	Enmedio	1504m
31	Encina	1496m
32	Lopera	1485m
33	Cisne	1483m
34	Alto Ubares	1399m
35	Buitrera	1378m
36	Chupa	1352m
37	Verde 1	1329m
38	Alto la Teja	1325m
39	Alto del Águila	1325m
40	Atalya	1255m
41	Pico del Puerto	1225m
42	Martos	1222m
43	Rodoceros	1207m
44	Tres Cruces	1204m
45	Panizo	1201m
46	Umbria de los Moriscos	1181m
47	Capriote	1145m
48	Naranjo	1140m
49	Escala	1108m
50	Mesa de Fornes	1080m
51	Gallego	1074m
52	Cizo	1070m
53	El Fuerte (nr La Maroma)	976m
54	Monderos	930m
55	Verde 2	918m

APPENDIX B
Wild mountain flowers of Andalucía

Common English name Spurge
Latin/Spanish name *Euphorbia/Euforbia*
Height 200–600mm
In bloom Early spring
Coverage Widespread
Elevation 300–1000m
Comments Poisonous

Common English name Stinking hellebore
Latin/Spanish name *Helleborus foetidus*
Height 500mm
In bloom April
Coverage La Maroma
Elevation 900–1300m
Comments Poisonous

Common English name Hedgehog broom
Latin/Spanish name *Abrojo/Piorno azul*
Height 400mm
In bloom April
Coverage La Maroma
Elevation 800–1000m

Common English name Sweet alyssum
Latin/Spanish name *Alyssum aizoides*
Height 100mm
In bloom April
Coverage La Maroma
Elevation 1000m

Appendix B – Wild mountain flowers of Andalucía

Common English name	Red-leafed rose
Latin/Spanish name	*Rosa glauca*
Height	175mm
In bloom	April
Coverage	La Maroma
Elevation	1200m
Comments	Vibrant red flower

Common English name	White cistus
Latin/Spanish name	*Estepa negra*
Height	Up to 2m
In bloom	April
Coverage	Widespread
Elevation	300–700m

Common English name	Rock rose
Latin/Spanish name	*Cistus/Flor de jara*
Height	Up to 1500mm
In bloom	March/April
Coverage	Widespread
Elevation	300–600m
Comments	Very delicate petals

Common English name	Petticoat daffodil
Latin/Spanish name	*Narciso*
Height	150mm
In bloom	March
Coverage	Almendrón
Elevation	350m

Common English name	Sage
Latin/Spanish name	*Salvia de montaña/mantagallo*
Height	1200mm
In bloom	Early April
Coverage	Widespread
Elevation	400–800m

THE MOUNTAINS AROUND NERJA

Common English name	Broom
Latin/Spanish name	*Lluvia de oro* (rain of gold)
Height	Up to 2500mm
In bloom	February to May
Coverage	Widespread
Elevation	Below 500m

Common English name	Crocus
Latin/Spanish name	*Azafrán*
Height	50–100mm
In bloom	February, again in October
Coverage	Widespread
Elevation	1200–2000m

Common English name	Fringed pink
Latin/Spanish name	*Dianthus superbus/clavelina*
Height	250mm
In bloom	March/April
Coverage	El Fuerte
Elevation	400m

Common English name	Kidney vetch
Latin/Spanish name	*Vulneraria*
Height	50–150mm
In bloom	February to April
Coverage	El Fuerte
Elevation	500m

Common English name	Lavender
Latin/Spanish name	*Cantueso/Azaya/Lavanda*
Height	800–1300mm
In bloom	March/April
Coverage	Valle de la Miel
Elevation	500–700m

Appendix B – Wild mountain flowers of Andalucía

Common English name	Common orchid
Latin/Spanish name	*Orquídea*
Height	150–225mm
In bloom	Early April
Coverage	El Chamizo
Elevation	1000m

Common English name	Giant asphodel
Latin/Spanish name	*Asphodelus fistulosus*
Height	500–1000mm
In bloom	Early April
Coverage	El Cielo and La Maroma
Elevation	1000–2000m

Common English name	Gum cistus/Gum rockrose
Latin/Spanish name	*Jara pringosa*
Height	Up to 2500mm
In bloom	April
Coverage	Widespread
Elevation	600–800m

Common English name	Purple orchid
Latin/Spanish name	*Orchis mascula*
Height	200mm
In bloom	Early April
Coverage	El Chamizo
Elevation	1000m

Common English name	Gladiolus
Latin/Spanish name	*Gladiolus*
Height	400–500mm
In bloom	March/April
Coverage	Valle de la Miel
Elevation	700m

The Mountains around Nerja

Common English name	Hare's ear
Latin/Spanish name	*Bupleurum*
Height	350mm
In bloom	April
Coverage	Valle de la Miel
Elevation	600m

Common English name	Spotted orchid
Latin/Spanish name	*Orquídea manchada*
Height	225mm
In bloom	Early April
Coverage	El Chamizo
Elevation	1000m

Common English name	Cytinus
Latin/Spanish name	*Teticas de doncella*
Height	50mm
In bloom	April
Coverage	Valle de la Miel
Elevation	700m
Comments	Parasite of cistus

Common English name	Wild clary
Latin/Spanish name	*Salvia*
Height	400mm
In bloom	April
Coverage	El Cielo
Elevation	900m

Common English name	Scrambling gromwell
Latin/Spanish name	*Glandora diffusa/Carrasquilla azul*
Height	125mm
In bloom	April
Coverage	El Cielo
Elevation	800m

Appendix B – Wild mountain flowers of Andalucía

Common English name	Blue iris
Latin/Spanish name	*Lirio azul*
Height	200mm
In bloom	March/April
Coverage	Widespread
Elevation	Below 300m

Common English name	Rosemary
Latin/Spanish name	*Romero*
Height	500–1500mm
In bloom	December to May
Coverage	Widespread
Elevation	300–800m
Comments	Edible, flavoursome

Common English name	Bindweed
Latin/Spanish name	*Convolvulus/Campanilla*
Height	30mm
In bloom	April/May
Coverage	El Cielo
Elevation	900m

Common English name	Rock soapwort
Latin/Spanish name	*Saponaria ocymoides*
Height	500mm
In bloom	April
Coverage	El Cielo
Elevation	700m

Common English name	Tassel grape hyacinth
Latin/Spanish name	*Leopoldia comosa*
Height	400mm
In bloom	April
Coverage	Below El Cielo
Elevation	450m

The Mountains around Nerja

Common English name	Blue grass lily
Latin/Spanish name	*Aphyllanthes monspeliensis/ Falso junquillo*
Height	150mm
In bloom	April
Coverage	El Cielo
Elevation	900m

Common English name	Candytuft
Latin/Spanish name	*Carraspique*
Height	300mm
In bloom	April
Coverage	La Maroma
Elevation	1200m

APPENDIX C
Glossary of useful Spanish words

Spanish	English
abandonada	disused, abandoned
altura	altitude
arroyo	stream
barranco	ravine
cabra	goat
calera	limestone quarry/kiln
camino	path, track
campo	field, country
cantera	quarry
cascada	waterfall
cazador	hunter
cerro	mountain, hill
collado	pass
cortijo	country farmhouse
cruz	cross
cuerda	string, rope
cuesta	hill, shoulder
cueva	cave
cuna	cradle, col
cuña	wedge
embalse	reservoir
encina	evergreen oak – holm oak
fuente	well, spring, fountain
haza	plot of arable land
goya	river basin, valley
llano	plain, area of flat ground
loma	hill, hillock
maroma	rope
mirador	vantage point, lookout
mojón	marker, boundary stone
nacimiento	birth, source (of a river)
peñón	crag, rocky outcrop
pozo	water well
pradillo	small meadow
prado	meadow
presa	dam
puerta	gate, door
puerto	a port, but in this case a mountain pass
rambla	dry riverbed, but also boulevard
raspón	groove or scrape (suggesting a track cut into the landscape)
refugio	refuge
sendero	path
tajo	face, cliff (rock face of a mountain)
venta	inn, hostelry

APPENDIX D
Further reading

Maps

Mapa Topográfico 1:50,000. These are the Spanish equivalent of Ordnance Survey maps. Four are required: 1040, 1041, 1054 and 1055. Not freely available. Can be purchased from Mapas y Compañíia, Málaga (on Calle Compañía). May also be purchased online. Poor quality paper.

Mapa Topográfico 1:25,000. Larger scale. The maps are gridded in metric, but also have the imperial outline in the margins. There are four maps to every one of the four 1:50,000 scale. That, therefore, is 16 maps to cover the entire area. For the walk to La Maroma from Alcaicería four maps will be needed. The quality of paper that the maps are printed on is poor, so that they have a limited lifespan. Have not been updated in 50 years.

Editorial Penebética Publish a 1:40,000 map that covers the area. It shows walks on the map and provides a booklet describing each walk (in Spanish only).

Piolet Very good map at a scale of 1:25,000. It comes in two sheets and shows 34 tracks, with no accompanying booklet.

Axarquía Tour and Trail 1:40,000. Published by Discovery Walking Guides, this is quite a clear map, but the October 2010 version has many little mistakes. Unfortunately, the 2010 version is to an imperial grid.

Discovery Tour and Trail 1:40,000. 2010 version issued with Charles Davis's walks on it. Imperial grid only. Very clear and easy to follow, but contains a number of minor errors.

Mapa Topográfico 1:75,000, Miguel Angel Torres Delgado 2002. Gridded in metric, but the detail is poor; paths and dirt tracks are difficult to follow.

Geological maps: the Instituto Geológico y Minero de España publish 1:200,000 maps of the Iberian Peninsula; the mountains around Nerja are within the scope of Map 83.

Appendix D – Further reading

Walking guides
Sierras de Tejeda, Almijara y Alhama, Manuel Clavero Salvador, Cornicabra, 2011. The official guide to the Axarquía region, in Spanish. Excellent publication. Very well illustrated. Maps included.

Gran Senda de Málaga para Todos, Diputación de Málaga. Free download from the website (www.gransendademalaga.es). 200 pages, with maps and itineraries. First published 2015.

La Axarquía – Land to the East of Málaga, Hilary Gavilan, Discovery Walking Guides, 2008. This book, in English, describes the history and culture of the Axarquía.

Flora and fauna
Flores Silvestres de Andalucía, Gabriel García Guardia, Editorial Rueda, 1988. A guide, in Spanish, to wildflowers, but mainly at low level. Well illustrated, but no cross references to northern European flowers.

Common Wildflowers of Spain, Austen F. Colwell, Santana, 2008. Few specific mountain flowers of Andalucía are included. Some of the flowers are cross referenced in Spanish.

APPENDIX E
Useful contacts

Contact details are listed below, with English-speaking services noted. Be aware that contact via email or phone is Spanish-language only – attempts made in English are likely to be ignored.

Tourist office
Located under the archway at the town side of the Balcón de Europa. They speak English.

Oficina de Turismo
Calle Carmen 1
Tel +34 952 5215 31
turismo@nerja.org

Hospital
Off the road north out of town, Avenida Ciudad de Pescia, half a kilometre beyond the bus station. Somebody there will be able to speak English.

Centro de Salud Nerja
Calle Carlos Millón, s/n
Tel +34 951 2896 62

Police
On the same road north, before the hospital. Unlikely to find anyone speaking English.

Policía Local de Nerja
Calle Virgen del Pilar, just off Avenida Ciudad de Pescia
Tel +34 9525 215 45

Appendix E – Useful contacts

Book/map shops
La Libreria in Plaza Cavana, near the Balcón de Europa, and Smiffs in Calle Almirante Ferrandiz. Both speak English.

Libreria Europa
Calle Granada 2
Tel +34 9525 206 39
www.libreriaeuropanerja.es/en

Smiffs
Calle Almirante Ferrandiz 10
Tel +34 9525 231 02

Post Office
On the same street as Smiffs. No English spoken.

Oficina de Correos
Calle Almirante Ferrandiz 6
Tel +34 9525 217 49

Accommodation
The best source of information on hotels, hostels and holiday lets in the area is www.nerjatoday.com/nerjaareaguide. All in English.

Weather
The best source for local weather forecasts is www.nerjatoday.com/nerjanews/nerja-weather

Taxi services
All taxi services speaking English advertise on www.nerjatoday.com/nerja/taxis

Local walking club
La Gineta Club de Montaña, club secretary Fernando Arce
(tel +34 609 5232 35 – Spanish language).

Walking guides
John Keo (www.hikingwalkingspain.com) or **Javier** (www.andalucianwalks.com). Both speak English.

DOWNLOAD THE GPX FILES

All the routes in this guide are available for download from:

www.cicerone.co.uk/1176/GPX

as standard format GPX files. You should be able to load them into most online GPX systems and mobile devices, whether GPS or smartphone. You may need to convert the file into your preferred format using a conversion programme such as gpsvisualizer.com or one of the many other such websites and programmes.

When you follow this link, you will be asked for your email address and where you purchased the guidebook, and have the option to subscribe to the Cicerone e-newsletter.

www.cicerone.co.uk

LISTING OF CICERONE GUIDES

BRITISH ISLES CHALLENGES, COLLECTIONS AND ACTIVITIES

Cycling Land's End to John o' Groats
Great Walks on the England Coast Path
The Big Rounds
The Book of the Bivvy
The Book of the Bothy
The Mountains of England and Wales: Vol 1 Wales
The Mountains of England and Wales: Vol 2 England
The National Trails
Walking the End to End Trail

SHORT WALKS SERIES

Short Walks Hadrian's Wall
Short Walks in Arnside and Silverdale
Short Walks in Cornwall: Falmouth and the Lizard
Short Walks in Dumfries and Galloway
Short Walks in Nidderdale
Short Walks in Pembrokeshire: Tenby and the south
Short Walks in the South Downs: Brighton, Eastbourne and Arundel
Short Walks in the Surrey Hills
Short Walks Lake District – Coniston and Langdale
Short Walks Lake District: Keswick, Borrowdale and Buttermere
Short Walks Lake District: Windermere Ambleside and Grasmere
Short Walks on the Malvern Hills
Short Walks Winchester

SCOTLAND

Ben Nevis and Glen Coe
Cycling in the Hebrides
Cycling the North Coast 500
Great Mountain Days in Scotland
Mountain Biking in Southern and Central Scotland
Mountain Biking in West and North West Scotland
Not the West Highland Way
Scotland
Scotland's Best Small Mountains
Scotland's Mountain Ridges
Scottish Wild Country Backpacking
Skye's Cuillin Ridge Traverse
The Borders Abbeys Way
The Great Glen Way
The Great Glen Way Map Booklet
The Hebridean Way
The Hebrides
The Isle of Mull
The Isle of Skye
The Skye Trail
The Southern Upland Way
The West Highland Way
The West Highland Way Map Booklet
Walking Ben Lawers, Rannoch and Atholl
Walking in the Cairngorms
Walking in the Pentland Hills
Walking in the Scottish Borders
Walking in the Southern Uplands
Walking in Torridon, Fisherfield, Fannichs and An Teallach
Walking Loch Lomond and the Trossachs
Walking on Arran
Walking on Harris and Lewis
Walking on Jura, Islay and Colonsay
Walking on Rum and the Small Isles
Walking on the Orkney and Shetland Isles
Walking on Uist and Barra
Walking the Cape Wrath Trail
Walking the Corbetts
  Vol 1 South of the Great Glen
  Vol 2 North of the Great Glen
Walking the Galloway Hills
Walking the John o' Groats Trail
Walking the Munros
  Vol 1 – Southern, Central and Western Highlands
  Vol 2 – Northern Highlands and the Cairngorms
Winter Climbs in the Cairngorms
Winter Climbs: Ben Nevis and Glen Coe

NORTHERN ENGLAND ROUTES

Cycling the Reivers Route
Cycling the Way of the Roses
Hadrian's Cycleway
Hadrian's Wall Path
Hadrian's Wall Path Map Booklet
The Coast to Coast Cycle Route
The Coast to Coast Walk
The Coast to Coast Walk Map Booklet
The Pennine Way
The Pennine Way Map Booklet
Walking the Dales Way
Walking the Dales Way Map Booklet

NORTH-EAST ENGLAND, YORKSHIRE DALES AND PENNINES

Cycling in the Yorkshire Dales
Great Mountain Days in the Pennines
Mountain Biking in the Yorkshire Dales
The Cleveland Way and the Yorkshire Wolds Way
The North York Moors
Trail and Fell Running in the Yorkshire Dales
Walking in County Durham
Walking in Northumberland
Walking in the North Pennines
Walking in the Yorkshire Dales:
  North and East
  South and West
Walking St Cuthbert's Way
Walking St Oswald's Way and Northumberland Coast Path

NORTH-WEST ENGLAND AND THE ISLE OF MAN

Cycling the Pennine Bridleway
Isle of Man Coastal Path
The Lancashire Cycleway
The Lune Valley and Howgills
Walking in Cumbria's Eden Valley
Walking in Lancashire
Walking in the Forest of Bowland and Pendle
Walking on the Isle of Man
Walking on the West Pennine Moors
Walking the Ribble Way
Walks in Silverdale and Arnside

LAKE DISTRICT

Bikepacking in the Lake District
Cycling in the Lake District
Great Mountain Days in the Lake District
Joss Naylor's Lakes, Meres and Waters of the Lake District
Lake District Winter Climbs
Lake District:
  High Level and Fell Walks
  Low Level and Lake Walks
Mountain Biking in the Lake District
Outdoor Adventures with Children – Lake District
Scrambles in the Lake District –
  North
  South
Trail and Fell Running in the Lake District
Walking The Cumbria Way
Walking the Lake District Fells –
  Borrowdale
  Buttermere
  Coniston
  Keswick
  Langdale
  Mardale and the Far East
  Patterdale
  Wasdale
Walking the Tour of the Lake District

DERBYSHIRE, PEAK DISTRICT AND MIDLANDS

Cycling in the Peak District
Dark Peak Walks
Scrambles in the Dark Peak

Walking in Derbyshire
Walking in the Peak District –
    White Peak East
    White Peak West

SOUTHERN ENGLAND

20 Classic Sportive Rides in
    South East England
    South West England
Cycling in the Cotswolds
Mountain Biking on the
    North Downs
    South Downs
Suffolk Coast and Heath Walks
The Cotswold Way
The Cotswold Way Map Booklet
The Kennet and Avon Canal
The Lea Valley Walk
The North Downs Way
The North Downs Way Map Booklet
The Peddars Way and Norfolk
    Coast Path
The Pilgrims' Way
The Ridgeway National Trail
The Ridgeway National Trail
    Map Booklet
The South Downs Way
The South Downs Way Map Booklet
The Thames Path
The Thames Path Map Booklet
The Two Moors Way
The Two Moors Way Map Booklet
Walking Hampshire's Test Way
Walking in Cornwall
Walking in Essex
Walking in Kent
Walking in London
Walking in Norfolk
Walking in the Chilterns
Walking in the Cotswolds
Walking in the Isles of Scilly
Walking in the New Forest
Walking in the North Wessex Downs
Walking on Dartmoor
Walking on Guernsey
Walking on Jersey
Walking on the Isle of Wight
Walking the Dartmoor Way
Walking the Jurassic Coast
Walking the South West Coast Path
Walking the South West Coast Path
    Map Booklets
    – Vol 1: Minehead to St Ives
    – Vol 2: St Ives to Plymouth
    – Vol 3: Plymouth to Poole
Walks in the South Downs
    National Park

WALES AND WELSH BORDERS

Cycle Touring in Wales
Cycling Lon Las Cymru
Great Mountain Days in Snowdonia
Hillwalking in Shropshire
Mountain Walking in Snowdonia
Offa's Dyke Path
Offa's Dyke Path Map Booklet
Ridges of Snowdonia
Scrambles in Snowdonia
Snowdonia: 30 Low-level and
    Easy Walks
    – North
    – South
The Cambrian Way
The Pembrokeshire Coast Path
The Pembrokeshire Coast Path
    Map Booklet
The Snowdonia Way
Walking Glyndwr's Way
Walking in Carmarthenshire
Walking in Pembrokeshire
Walking in the Brecon Beacons
Walking in the Forest of Dean
Walking in the Wye Valley
Walking on Gower
Walking the Severn Way
Walking the Shropshire Way
Walking the Wales Coast Path

INTERNATIONAL CHALLENGES, COLLECTIONS AND ACTIVITIES

Europe's High Points
Walking the Via Francigena
    Pilgrim Route – Part 1

AFRICA

Kilimanjaro
Walking in the Drakensberg
Walks and Scrambles in the
    Moroccan Anti-Atlas

ALPS CROSS-BORDER ROUTES

100 Hut Walks in the Alps
Alpine Ski Mountaineering
    Vol 1 – Western Alps
The Karnischer Hohenweg
The Tour of the Bernina
Trail Running – Chamonix and the
    Mont Blanc region
Trekking Chamonix to Zermatt
Trekking in the Alps
Trekking in the Silvretta and
    Ratikon Alps
Trekking Munich to Venice
Trekking the Tour du Mont Blanc
Trekking the Tour du Mont Blanc
    Map Booklet
Walking in the Alps

PYRENEES AND FRANCE/SPAIN CROSS-BORDER ROUTES

Shorter Treks in the Pyrenees
The Pyrenean Haute Route
The Pyrenees
Trekking the GR11 Trail
Walks and Climbs in the Pyrenees

AUSTRIA

Innsbruck Mountain Adventures
Trekking Austria's Adlerweg
Trekking in Austria's Hohe Tauern
Trekking in Austria's Zillertal Alps
Trekking in the Stubai Alps
Walking in Austria
Walking in the Salzkammergut:
    the Austrian Lake District

EASTERN EUROPE

The Danube Cycleway Vol 2
The High Tatras
The Mountains of Romania
Walking in Hungary

FRANCE, BELGIUM AND LUXEMBOURG

Camino de Santiago – Via Podiensis
Chamonix Mountain Adventures
Cycle Touring in France
Cycling London to Paris
Cycling the Canal de la Garonne
Cycling the Canal du Midi
Cycling the Route des Grandes Alpes
Mont Blanc Walks
Mountain Adventures in
    the Maurienne
Short Treks on Corsica
The Elbe Cycle Route
The GR5 Trail
The GR5 Trail – Benelux and
    Lorraine
The GR5 Trail – Vosges and Jura
The Grand Traverse of the
    Massif Central
The Moselle Cycle Route
The River Loire Cycle Route
The River Rhone Cycle Route
Trekking in the Vanoise
Trekking the Cathar Way
Trekking the GR10
Trekking the GR20 Corsica
Trekking the Robert Louis
    Stevenson Trail
Via Ferratas of the French Alps
Walking in Provence – East
Walking in Provence – West
Walking in the Ardennes
Walking in the Auvergne
Walking in the Briançonnais
Walking in the Dordogne
Walking in the Haute Savoie: North
Walking in the Haute Savoie: South
Walking on Corsica
Walking the Brittany Coast Path

GERMANY

Hiking and Cycling in the
    Black Forest
The Danube Cycleway Vol 1
The Rhine Cycle Route
The Westweg
Walking in the Bavarian Alps

IRELAND
The Wild Atlantic Way and Western Ireland
Walking the Wicklow Way

ITALY
Alta Via – Trekking in the Dolomites – Vols 1&2
Day Walks in the Dolomites
Italy's Grande Traversata delle Alpi
Italy's Sibillini National Park
Ski Touring and Snowshoeing in the Dolomites
The Way of St Francis
Trekking in the Apennines
Trekking the Giants' Trail: Alta Via 1 through the Italian Pennine Alps
Via Ferratas of the Italian Dolomites – Vols 1&2
Walking in Abruzzo
Walking in Italy's Cinque Terre
Walking in Italy's Stelvio National Park
Walking in Sicily
Walking in the Aosta Valley
Walking in the Dolomites
Walking in Tuscany
Walking in Umbria
Walking Lake Como and Maggiore
Walking Lake Garda and Iseo
Walking on the Amalfi Coast
Walking the Via Francigena Pilgrim Route – Parts 2&3
Walks and Treks in the Maritime Alps

MEDITERRANEAN
The High Mountains of Crete
Trekking in Greece
Walking and Trekking in Zagori
Walking and Trekking on Corfu
Walking in Cyprus
Walking on Malta
Walking on the Greek Islands – the Cyclades

NEW ZEALAND AND AUSTRALIA
Hiking the Overland Track

NORTH AMERICA
Hiking and Cycling the California Missions Trail
The John Muir Trail
The Pacific Crest Trail

SOUTH AMERICA
Aconcagua and the Southern Andes
Hiking and Biking Peru's Inca Trails
Trekking in Torres del Paine

SCANDINAVIA, ICELAND AND GREENLAND
Hiking in Norway – South
Trekking in Greenland – The Arctic Circle Trail
Trekking the Kungsleden
Walking and Trekking in Iceland

SLOVENIA, CROATIA, SERBIA, MONTENEGRO AND ALBANIA
Hiking Slovenia's Juliana Trail
Mountain Biking in Slovenia
The Islands of Croatia
The Julian Alps of Slovenia
The Mountains of Montenegro
The Peaks of the Balkans Trail
The Slovene Mountain Trail
Walking in Slovenia: The Karavanke
Walks and Treks in Croatia

SPAIN AND PORTUGAL
Camino de Santiago: Camino Frances
Coastal Walks in Andalucia
Costa Blanca Mountain Adventures
Cycling the Camino de Santiago
Cycling the Ruta Via de la Plata
Mountain Walking in Mallorca
Mountain Walking in Southern Catalunya
Portugal's Rota Vicentina
Spain's Sendero Historico: The GR1
The Andalucian Coast to Coast Walk
The Camino del Norte and Camino Primitivo
The Camino Ingles and Ruta do Mar
The Camino Portugues
The Mountains Around Nerja
The Mountains of Ronda and Grazalema
The Sierras of Extremadura
Trekking in Mallorca
Trekking in the Canary Islands
Trekking the GR7 in Andalucia
Walking and Trekking in the Sierra Nevada
Walking in Andalucia
Walking in Catalunya – Barcelona
Walking in Catalunya – Girona Pyrenees
Walking in Portugal
Walking in the Algarve
Walking in the Picos de Europa
Walking La Via de la Plata and Camino Sanabres
Walking on Gran Canaria
Walking on La Gomera and El Hierro
Walking on La Palma
Walking on Lanzarote and Fuerteventura
Walking on Madeira
Walking on Tenerife
Walking on the Azores
Walking on the Costa Blanca
Walking the Camino dos Faros

SWITZERLAND
Switzerland's Jura Crest Trail
The Swiss Alps
Tour of the Jungfrau Region
Trekking the Swiss Via Alpina
Walking in the Bernese Oberland – Jungfrau region
Walking in the Engadine – Switzerland
Walking in the Valais
Walking in Ticino
Walking in Zermatt and Saas-Fee

CHINA, JAPAN AND ASIA
Hiking and Trekking in the Japan Alps and Mount Fuji
Hiking in Hong Kong
Japan's Kumano Kodo Pilgrimage
Trekking in Tajikistan

HIMALAYA
Annapurna
8000 metres
Everest: A Trekker's Guide
Trekking in Bhutan
Trekking in Ladakh
Trekking in the Himalaya
Trekking in the Karakoram

MOUNTAIN LITERATURE
A Walk in the Clouds
Abode of the Gods
Fifty Years of Adventure
The Pennine Way – the Path, the People, the Journey
Unjustifiable Risk?
Unjustifiable Risk?

TECHNIQUES
Fastpacking
Geocaching in the UK
Map and Compass
Outdoor Photography
The Mountain Hut Book

MINI GUIDES
Alpine Flowers
Navigation
Pocket First Aid and Wilderness Medicine
Snow

For full information on all our guides, books and eBooks,
visit our website:
www.cicerone.co.uk

CICERONE

Trust Cicerone to guide your next adventure, wherever it may be around the world…

Discover guides for hiking, mountain walking, backpacking, trekking, trail running, cycling and mountain biking, ski touring, climbing and scrambling in Britain, Europe and worldwide.

Connect with Cicerone online and find inspiration.

- buy books and ebooks
- articles, advice and trip reports
- podcasts and live events
- GPX files and updates
- regular newsletter

cicerone.co.uk